LET YOUR INTUITIVE MIND TOUCH THE VISION. . .

Most people feel there is a power greater than themselves. We witness miracles in our daily lives. Many feel guided by a divine force and grasp the idea that life is eternal. However or whatever words we use to describe our inner knowing of Infinite Love, it is with us always, it is"beyond words."

Beyond Words

According to many, we are at the birth of a New Age, an age of awareness and acceptance of forms of being and of consciousness that go beyond the realm of the physical or even the mental, into metaphysical, intuitive, psychic and spiritual dimensions.

As changes occur in our society, the language used to describe it evolves; new words are coined, old words and phrases take on different meanings.

Beyond Words is an invaluable reference book for anyone seeking to know more about the New Age and its concepts.

E. J. Klages, author
Taking the Waters

Reality is shaped by our words. Let us unfold a new language of terms for transforming consciousness. "Let us stop measuring eternity with an hourglass and infinity with a yardstick."

Paula B. Slater
Barbara   Sinor

Beyond Words

Terms for Transforming Consciousness

Paula B. Slater, M.A.
Barbara Sinor, M.A.

Published by
Harbin Springs Publishing
 P. O. Box 1132
Middletown, CA 95461

Library of Congress Cataloging-in-Publication Data

Slater, Paula B., 1952-
    Beyond Words : terms for transforming consciousness / by Paula B.
  Slater and Barbara Sinor.
       p.   cm.
    Includes bibliographical references.
      ISBN 0-944202-05-5 : $14.95 (est.)
      1. Occultism — Terminology. 2. Parapsychology — Terminology.
    3. New Age movement — Terminology.   I. Sinor, Barbara, 1945-
    II. Title.
    BF1411.s56 1990
     133—dc20

This book is dedicated to
Mom and Dad
whose liberal guidance and loving faith
opened our minds and lighted our path
to spiritual awakening.

ACKNOWLEDGEMENTS

We wish to acknowledge our many relatives and friends who have supported our writing adventures over the years. Your ceaseless patience and attentive ear to listen "just one more time" to changes and rewrites is admirable.

Also, we thank Willis Harman for making room in his busy schedule to honor our book with a Foreword; Stanley Krippner for his valuable suggestions and expertise; Juanita Emery for listening to her intuition in guiding us to our publisher and for proofreading with a keen eye; Chris Slater and David Sinor for their thoughtful advice and unwavering encouragement.

A special acknowledgement is extended to Becky, Sherry, and the wonderful staff at Harbin Springs Publishing. Libby and Tim, your hard work and dedication to professionalism and to creating our vision into a reality is deeply appreciated; Hilarie, thank you for your enthusiastic marketing efforts and support.

We express gratitude to all the courageous men and women who have braved the way for this awakening New Age. Our history is rich with forward-thinking individuals who have touched the magic of spirit and who shared their discoveries with us. We celebrate the insights and wisdom of a few of these visionaries through a selection of quotes.

Lastly, we acknowledge and thank our "higher guiding forces" who have shown us a world beyond words and continue to inspire our writing and our lives.

Foreword

Something revolutionary is happening in the world. Deeper than the revolutionary coming together of the European Community, quieter but more fundamental than the breathtaking revolutions toward liberty and democracy in Eastern Europe, related to the spread of "Green thinking" in Europe and the "deep ecology" and radical feminist movements in the United States, it is a wave of profound cultural change—more profound than anything the Western world has known for several centuries at least.

One of the terms sometimes applied to this wave of change is "New Age." "New Age" is a term toward which there are a range of reactions, and of which there are a variety of interpretations. Whether you feel yourself to be a part of it or mildly repelled, whether you are an avid enthusiast or disinterested bystander — even if you feel hostile to it and find it threatening to the well-being of society — clarity of definition is certainly desirable, so at least when we discuss or evaluate, we are talking about the same thing.

To some, "New Age" connotes crystals, horoscopes, psychic phenomena, pyramid power, and some queer sort of faddish fascination with superstitious nonsense that educated people discarded after the scientific revolution. But of course many who display an interest in these "New Age" topics are well schooled, and quite aware that their interests fly in the face of the prevailing materialist scientific world view.

Earlier in this century that materialist view was pitted against the remnants of the world view of Christendom, in a conflict billed as "the warfare between science and religion." In my own graduate student days it was generally assumed that the war had ended and that science had won, hands down.

However, since the 1960s there has been a renewal of the action, and this time it is reductionistic science that is on the defensive against spreading interest in meditative spiritual practices and other explorations. The attack is strengthened by growing disenchantment with some of the consequences of technological application unguided by suitable values. As theologian Jacob Needleman wrote in his introductory paragraph to *A Sense of the Cosmos* (1975):

> *Once the hope of mankind, modern science has now become the object of such mistrust and disappointment that it will*

probably never again speak with its old authority. [The problems contributed to by modern technologies have] eroded what was once a general trust in the goodness of science. And the appearance in our society of alien metaphysical systems, of "new religions" sourced in the East, and of ideas and fragments of teachings emanating from ancient times have all contributed doubt about the truth of science. Even among scientists themselves there are signs of a metaphysical rebellion.

Using a different metaphor, Thomas Berry has written about how we are searching for a "New Story"—a new account of how things came to be as they are, an account within which we find a sense of life purpose, a guide to education, an understanding of our suffering, and impetus for energized action. It is apparent to more and more people that the Old Story has become fragmented and nonfunctional. At the heart of the "New Story" will be, clearly, the insight of science and the facts of evolution. But that story, as it is told in our science classrooms, is incomplete, and in its incompleteness, distorting. It has displaced the old but not matured sufficiently to serve as the new. So the "New Story" will include science and evolutionary development (without the faith in natural selection as the sole mechanism); but it will account for a far broader range of human experience—including particularly those kinds of experience in which we most clearly show ourselves as distinctly human.

When the order of Western European society was being shaken by the scientific heresy, in the seventeenth century, one of the manifestations was a variety of social movements which in themselves were disturbing. There were the Quakers and the Shakers, the Diggers and the Levellers and the Muggletonians, and many more. They were disturbing because of their heretical or political beliefs, and their uncouth appearance with their beards and strange costumes, and their unconventional interests and lifestyles. We have more or less forgotten about them, but they were the seventeenth-century equivalent of various "New Age" groups in recent times.

Because this too is a time of heresy, and heresy tends to spawn such behaviors and groupings. The "new heresy" questions the orthodoxy of materialistic science, and challenges the basic metaphysical assumptions on which modern industrial society was based. So whatever our initial feelings about this "New Age craze" (as some would call it), because of its historical significance we need to be knowledgeable about it.

And what better way to be knowledgeable about the emerging "New Story" than through a brief encyclopedia with short articles on key terms! That is what these authors have provided —*Beyond Words* is informative and relevant, and entertaining as well.

Willis Harman, Ph. D.
President, Institute of Noetic Sciences
Sausalito, California

Introduction

> *There is a way of knowing that is only awareness.*
> *And because what was experienced was not experienced in*
> *words; it cannot be remembered or told or even reexperienced*
> *in words.*
>
> Lawrence Kushner, *Honey from the Rock [1977]*

A Victorian Fantasy entitled *Flatland* describes a two-dimensional world of geometric shaped beings and illustrates the limitation of language. The story begins when the main character, a middle-aged square, has a nightmare of a one-dimensional realm, Lineland, where the inhabitants move only from point to point. He tries to explain to the Linelanders his own two-dimensional world in which beings can move from side to side as well as from point to point, but they find his description incomprehensible and are about to attack him when he awakens.

Soon after this dream his grandson, little Hexagon, needing help with his homework suggests the possibility of a third dimension. The Square scoffs at his grandson's notion of not only a side to side but also an up and down reality.

That night the Square is visited by a being from Spaceland, a three-dimensional world. This transformational encounter with a circle — who isn't a circle as he knows it — terribly confuses the Square:

> *I saw a line that was no Line; Space that was not Space.....*
> *"Either this is madness or it is Hell."*
>
> *"It is neither," calmly replied the Sphere. "It is knowledge; it*
> *is Three Dimensions. Open your eyes once again and try to*
> *look steadily."*

The Square then sets out to share with his fellow Flatlanders that Space is more than just a wild notion of mathematicians. The Chief Circle, who is also high priest of Flatland, finally has the Square imprisoned for the "public good."

This tale is a metaphor for the current confusion and shifting concerns of our present leap in awareness. When one reaches beyond the limiting framework of our linear world to test the stars, one not only threatens the beliefs of the norm, but is challenged to describe in linear terms a nonlinear experience. Fourth dimensional states including true "higher" states of consciousness do exist, but verbal communication about them is difficult: These experiences are *beyond words.*

Almost everyone has, at one time or another, touched a state of expanded awareness. In his book *Quantum Questions,* Ken Wilber writes, "Mystics universally speak of contacting reality in its "suchness," its "isness," its "thatness," without intermediaries; beyond words, symbols, names, thoughts, images." Although mere words do not suffice to describe such experiences, language is our main form of communication and thus our reality is shaped by words. Words are symbols which initiate a feeling, thought, or image, they are pillars supporting the truths found beyond words.

Language is an art form; an important transformative string to tug upon to gently pull our New Age paradigm into view. When words become language they, in turn, become a tool for developing a bond with reality. However, we must also look between the lines, beyond the words, to allow the intuitive mind to touch the vision. Greater understanding of this nonlinear reality will ultimately shape our vocabulary. The New Age is evolving a language to accommodate a world in transformation. The gaps in our use of language today provide the space to create new *terms for transforming consciousness.*

Carlos Castenada's, Don Juan said, "Seeing happens when one sneaks between the worlds." *Beyond Words,* written to entertain and enlighten, is an encyclopedia and a reference book of New Thought terms to help one see between the worlds. This book may be a starting place for some, an affirmation for others. In either case, it can be used as a tool to reach higher levels of awareness in the virtually unexplored areas of inner space.

Each subject or term in *Beyond Words* contains enough information to initiate your further study in areas which attract or fascinate you. The words, interconnected concepts, and philosophies defined here all have one thing in common: Each can contribute to a greater understanding of one's innate psychic and spiritual qualities. By providing a list of reference books at the end of each topic, we invite you to venture onward and inward.

Many mysteries await our inquiry: Quantum theory, miraculous healings, mounting ecological concerns, psychokenesis, thousands of reported near-death and out-of-body-experiences, and vast realms of unanswered questions. These mysteries beckon us to search beyond our linear realities. Extensive research performed in the fields of parapsychology and a shift in consciousness towards a metaphysical view are all indicative of our coming of age. Along with this transformative shift comes a current and growing focus on personal spirituality and humanitarianism.

We are at the center of an unwinding paradigm and great numbers of people are becoming aware that our existence consists of far more than eyes can see or conscious minds can reach. At this moment, we possess all that is needed to unlock our spiritual-selves and intuitive abilities — everything required to answer every question. Innocence, ignorance, and fear have shrouded these inherent gifts. *Beyond Words* attempts to bring them into the light of one's own brilliant and limitless reflection.

Paula B. Slater
Barbara Sinor

1990, The Year of Awakening

Table of Contents

Thought Games

"Richard, do you want to know the answer to
floating wrenches in the air and healing all sickness
and turning water into wine and walking on the waves
and landing Travel Airs on a hundred feet of grass?
Do you want to know the answer to all these
miracles?... This world? And everything in it? Illusions, Richard! Every bit of it Illusions!..."
If that's all illusion, Mister Shimoda, then what is
real? And if this life is illusion, why do we live at all?"

Richard Bach, *Illusions*

Affirmations

AFFIRMATIONS are positive statements which explain, state, or declare a desire. Affirmations require the sayer's belief that the desire will be fulfilled, and appropriate action taken toward that fulfillment. Affirmations work best (certainly fastest) in conjunction with positive action.

Let us say, you have always wanted to be a writer. Your affirmation could be: "I am becoming the best writer I can possibly be." Such a positive statement, and an effort to learn and practice the art of writing, puts one on the way toward achieving that goal.

Successful Affirmations require daily repetition and the *belief* that the process will succeed. Without that belief, the law of "ask and you shall receive" will not generate enough positive energy to manifest the stated desire and the Affirmation is incomplete. Affirmations are based on the principle that the subconscious mind is always awake, listening, and actively manifesting thoughts, speech, feeling and imagination. A more positive reality is created through the ongoing process of positive thinking, Affirmation, declaration, and ultimately, reception.

In her popular book, *What You Think of Me Is None of My Business,* Terry Cole-Whittaker explains, "The words you speak become your personal law because of the creative power of the subconscious. Listen to what you say and think. Become conscious of the cause behind the results in your life."

Many people use restrictive language without realizing it. Expressions such as "I'm so tired today," or "How am I going to pay all these bills?" or "I just hate my hair (eyes, nose, legs)," and "I *can't* do that!" are negative input to the subconscious mind. When you find yourself using negative statements, simply cut off the sentence or thought and re-create it as an Affirmation of your health, abundance, creativity, or anything positive.

Centering on a specific area of your life, hold in your mind what you want to accomplish. Think it, state it aloud, feel it. Always stay focused on the most positive outcome. Then *act* on it. Affirming without action is like chewing without swallowing.

Use Affirmations daily. State them in the present tense, and be specific: "I am using all my thoughts and concentration, my words, feelings, and actions to complete four good pages of this short story by the end of the day." The consequence of stating exactly your desire every day, and acting on the motivation thus created, fulfills the Affirmation and achieves the desired results.

When each day becomes an expression of your Affirmations, branch out by employing Affirmations of a broader scope: "My life's direction is toward becoming a successfully published writer." Addressing the big issue of career goals, once you have achieved the smaller issue of writing an article or short story, advances you several giant steps toward your long-term objective.

Recommended Reading

Cole-Whittaker, Terry. *What You Think of Me Is None of My Business.* New York: Rawson Associates, 1983. Best expresses and utilizes the technique of using Affirmations.

Gawain, Shakti. *Reflections in the Light.* San Rafael, CA: New World Library, 1988. Daily thoughts and Affirmations.

Hay, Louise L. *You Can Heal Your Life.* Santa Monica, CA: Hay House, Inc., 1984.

Shinn, Florence Scovel. *Word is Your Wand.* Los Angeles, CA: DeVorss & Co., 1928.

Shinn, Florence Scovel. *Power of the Spoken Word.* Los Angeles, CA: DeVorss & Co., 1945.

Collective Unconscious

> *The COLLECTIVE UNCONSCIOUS is the repository of myths, archetypes, universal race memory, and other images which link and interconnect everything in the Universe.*

Mystics refer to the Collective Unconscious as the Tao. In esoteric (see ESOTERIC) teachings it is called the Akashic Records, or Hall of Records. Famous psychotherapist and philosopher, Carl Jung, coined the term Collective Unconscious for the deeper layers of memory, or the archetypal layer of consciousness. Jung recognized, as did Freud, that we each have a personal unconscious containing our forgotten or repressed personal experiences. He also felt that we are continuously bathed in a sea of *collective consciousness.*

The Collective Unconscious is a universal memory bank, a cosmic record written throughout all time and space. Jung believed its contents contained primordial images which are the basis of man's thinking — the whole treasure-house of "mythological motifs." We have access to this Universal Mind (or social memory complex) through dreams, intuition, channeling, synchronicities, and flashes of inspiration (see Individual Headings).

The individual psyche is not isolated, it is part of a greater wholeness that enriches and connects us all. When the Roman poet Terence stated, "Nothing human is foreign to me," he was in touch with this larger inclusive mind with its inborn mythology and archetypal images common to all humanity.

Recommended Readings

Campbell, Joseph. *The Power of Myth.* New York: Doubleday, 1988. One of a kind.

Jung, C.G. *The Archetypes and the Collective Unconscious.* Princeton, NJ: Princeton University Press, reprinted 1980.

Cosmology

Cosmology

COSMOLOGY *is the study of the universe including theories about its origin, evolution, structure, and future. Specific study of the origin of the universe and of astronomical systems is called Cosmogony.*

The earliest Cosmological theories date back to 4000 B.C. with the Mesopotamian belief that the Earth was the center of the universe. Not until 1543 did Polish astronomer, Nicolaus Copernicus, challenge this theory proposing that the Earth revolved around the sun, and therefore could not be the center of the universe. In 1948 George Gamow, a Russian-American physicist, postulated the "Big-Bang Theory." This Cosmological model hypothesized that the universe began as the result of a gigantic explosion in outerspace — that all energy mass was created in one cataclysmic instant. According to this theory, and astronomical observation, the universe is still expanding outward from the origin of this creational explosion.

At present, the Big-Bang Theory remains the dominant Cosmological model in scientific circles. Astrophysicists believe that between fifteen and twenty billion years ago all matter known to exist was packed into an unimaginably dense "singularity." They further conjecture the possibility that gravity will one day draw the exploded matter back together. This would likely create yet another cosmic blast and begin the cycle once again—the repeated death and rebirth of the cosmos.

Long before contemporary cosmologists postulated these expansion/contraction cycles of creation they were described with astonishing accuracy in the scriptures of the Hindu religion. In the early inspired writings of the *Upanishads,* these cosmic reincarnating cycles are referred to as "the Breath of Brahma" — the expanding exhalation and the contracting inhalation of the God Force. This universal rhythm of expansion/contraction is also expressed in an ancient Chinese saying, "the yang, having reached its climax, retreats in favor of the yin" (see YIN/YANG, ANIMA/ANIMUS). The "fiery" expansions and gravitational compressions reported in ancient teachings were said to occur on a time scale of thousands of millions of years. This time frame falls within the same scale calculated by modern astrophysicists!

Since the development of the Big-Bang Theory, the uncertainty principle, the theory of relativity, and quantum physics (see QUANTUM PHYSICS), the Cosmological overview held by theoretical physicists and mathematicians has come to look suspiciously like that of the ancient mystics. Many scientists have discussed this similarity at length in their own work. Sir James Jeans, a mathematician, physicist, and astronomer, writes in, *The Mysterious Universe,* "God is a mathematician, and the universe begins to look more like a great thought than a great machine." "Universal energy" as the basis of *all* matter has fast become the center of scientific creational thought. Long before science was born, this Divine Plan of "the One in the Many," or God within all things, lived at the heart of mystical revelation.

Recommended Reading

Davies, Paul. *The Cosmic Blueprint: New Discoveries in Nature's Creative Ability to Order the Universe.* New York: Simon & Schuster, Inc., 1988.

Ferris,Timothy. *The Coming of Age in the Milky Way.* New York: William Morrow & Co., 1988. Absorbing.

Griffin, David Ray, editor. *The Reenchantment of Science: Postmodern Proposals.* Albany, NY: SUNY Press, 1987. Inclusions by David Bohm, Willis Harman, Rupert Sheldrake, and Stanley Krippner.

Hawking, Stephen W. *A Brief History of Time: From the Big Bang to Black Holes.* New York: Bantam Books, 1988. Written by a man who is widely regarded as the most brilliant theoretical physicist since Einstein.

Weinberg, Steven. *The First 3 Minutes.* New York: Bantam Books, 1982. Nobel Prize-winning physicist's view of the origin of the universe.

Creativity

> *CREATIVITY is a fluid and spontaneous reach of the mind that allows something new to enter the world. It is an act of doing and being, creatively.*

It is difficult to distinguish between intuition, imagination, mystical religious experience, and Creativity (see Individual Headings). Images are stored in the unconscious mind and flash into conscious awareness through Creative reverie states, nightly dreams, illuminations, visions, fantasies, and daydreams. These experiences originate from the same inner fabric of one's being; it is often impossible to tell where one takes off and another one begins.

Author Robert Masters found in his research with artists that levels are reached in the Creative process where the experience of the artist and the experience of the religious visionary cannot be differentiated from one another. Plato spoke of artists and poets when he wrote that it is "God himself who speaks and addresses us through them." And nineteenth century romantic poet Percy Shelley said, "A poet participates in the eternal, the infinite, and one."

Most renowned writers and musicians have at one time or another stated that their Creative work felt more like automatic writing (see INSPIRATIONAL/AUTOMATIC WRITING) or taking clairaudient (see CLAIRVOYANCE/CLAIRAUDIENCE) dictation than originating in their own minds. Acclaimed novelist Thomas Wolfe, complained of feeling "possessed" during his most Creative periods and Picasso acknowledged the aid of an invisible collaborator. Writer-philosopher Freidrich Nietzsche, declared that he felt invaded by an uncontrollable flood of Creativity. He wrote, "One can hardly reject completely the idea that one is the mere incarnation, or mouthpiece, or medium of some almighty power.... One takes; one does not ask who gives."

A state of relaxed awareness and ample time for incubation of ideas and inspiration seems to encourage Creative insight. In 1789, composer Wolfgang Mozart wrote to a friend, "When I am, as it were, completely myself, entirely alone, and of good cheer — say traveling in a carriage, or working after a good meal, or during the night when I cannot sleep; it is on such occasions that my ideas flow best and most abundantly..." Although creative activity engages communication between one's conscious and unconscious and appears to primarily involve the right hemisphere of the brain, scientists have found that it also draws on knowledge, logic, imagination, intuition, and the talent to form connections between concepts.

One of the most profound expressions of Creativity is a child fancifully dreaming up a make-believe reality. This innate magic to create can melt into every area of one's life. The highly Creative person sees the subdued colors cast in a shadow; enriches a letter with humor; finds adventure in a trip to the grocery store for a carton of milk; and enjoys cultivating relationships with imagination. Through Creative expression each moment becomes an extension of individual uniqueness.

In his insightful book, *The Courage to Create*, celebrated author and psychotherapist Rollo May writes:

> *Creativity must be seen in the work of the scientist as well as in that of the artist, in the thinker as well as in the aesthetician; and one must not rule out the extent to which it is present in captains of modern technology as well as in a mother's normal relationship with her child.*

We are all creators, inventors, artists. We are but a medium, an instrument through which the Universal Mind expresses itself. Through each of us, God is saying "I will create."

Recommended Reading

Edwards, Betty. *Drawing on the Right Side of the Brain.* Los Angeles: J.P. Tarcher, Inc., 1979.

Gardner, Howard. *Art, Mind and Brain.* New York: Basic Books, Inc., 1982. A cognitive approach to creativity.

Ghiselin, Brewster, editor. *The Creative Process.* New York: The New American Library, 1952. A rich anthology of thirty-eight brilliantly creative people — including Albert Einstein, Vincent Van Gogh, Carl Jung, W.B. Yeats, and Friedrich Nietzsche — and their thoughts on the creative process.

Harman, Willis, and Howard Rheingold. *Higher Creativity.* Los Angeles: J.P. Tarcher, Inc., 1984. Absolutely illuminating.

Hills, Christopher. *Creative Imagination.* Boulder Creek, CA: University of the Trees Press, 1986.

Klauser, Henriette Anne. *Writing on Both Sides of the Brain.* New York: Harper & Row, 1986. Breakthrough techniques for people who write.

May, Rollo. *The Courage to Create.* New York: W.W. Norton, 1975. One of the best books exploring the creative process.

Nierenberg, Gerard I. *The Art of Creative Thinking.* New York: Simon & Schuster, Inc., 1982. Provides exercises to increase one's creative thinking skills.

Death

DEATH......there is no such thing.

The word *death* implies finality, "the end of life" — that humans have a finite existence. Looking beyond the words, however, we find eternity. Humans experience the "act" of death, dying. This is the psychological framework that we accept. The steps, or stages of dying (disbelief, anger, depression, acceptance) are typical for many losses we incur throughout our lives. Renowned expert on the issues of death and dying, Elizabeth Kübler-Ross, expressed in a seminar, "Death does not exist..."

> *Death is simply a shedding of the physical body like the butterfly coming out of a cocoon. It is a transition into a higher state of consciousness, where you continue to perceive, to understand, to laugh, to be able to grow, and the only thing that you lose is something that you don't need anymore, and that is your physical body.*

We tend to talk in terms of the *physical* body's completion. We use words like "no pulse," "stopped beating," and "not breathing" to describe death. Words, however, exclude the spiritual nature of death.

Kahlil Gibran wrote in his masterpiece, *The Prophet*, "...life and death are one, even as the river and the sea are one." Below is a "true" story of a twelve year old girl who experienced a near-death experience (see NEAR-DEATH EXPERIENCE).

> *A twelve year old girl did not want to share with her mother that it was such a beautiful experience when she died, (later resuscitated) because no mommy likes to hear that her children found a place that's nicer than home; that's very understandable. But she had such a unique experience that she needed desperately to share it with somebody, and so one day she confided in her father. She told her father that it was such a beautiful experience when she died that she did not want to come back. What made it very special, besides the whole atmosphere and the fantastic love and light that most of them (those who experience a NDE) convey, was that her brother*

was there with her, and held her with great tenderness, love, and compassion. After sharing this she said to her father, "The only problem is that I don't have a brother." Then the father started to cry, and confessed that she indeed did have a brother who died about three months before she was born, but they had never told her.

Recommended Reading

Bliss, Raymond. *The Other Side of Death.* New York: University Books, 1971. Research material dealing with life after death.

Evans-Wentz, W.Y., editor. *The Tibetan Book of the Dead.* New York: Oxford University Press, 1960.

Kübler-Ross, Elizabeth. *Death: The Final Stage of Growth.* New York: Touchstone Books, 1986. Dealing with fears.

Kübler-Ross, Elizabeth. *On Death and Dying.* New York: Macmillan, 1970. A classic on the subject of death and dying.

Levine, Stephen. *Healing into Life and Death.* New York: Anchor Press/Doubleday, 1987. A vision of healing into death.

Meltzer, David, editor. *Death: An Anthology of Ancient Texts, Songs, Prayers, and Stories.* Berkeley: North Point Press, 1984. Exploring the meaning of death in many cultures and ages.

Osis, Karlis, and Erlendur Haraldson. *At the Hour of Death.* Hastings Press, 1986. A look at the near-death experience.

Roberts, Jane. *Emir's Education in the Proper Use of Magical Powers.* Walpole, NH: Stillpoint Publishing, 1984. A story of a prince that lived before "death" was invented.

Destiny

DESTINY is a cognate of the term destination and implies a direction or goal in life. The blueprint of personal Destiny is an interplay of one's inborn talents, socialization, genetics, race, gender, conscious choices, subconscious programming, and karmic possibilities.

During the Italian Renaissance, it was believed that God bestowed each creature with a particular quality and, therefore, a certain Destiny. To the fox He gave cunning, fidelity to the dog, and to the lion He gave strength. Finally, God came to the human being and decided to give him an open Destiny, implying "free will." In Dorothy Sayers' translation of the *Divine Comedy*, "Hell," God announced to humankind:

I created you as a being neither mortal nor immortal, neither heavenly nor earthly, so that you, as a sovereign and free artificer, could mold and forge yourself in the shape you choose. You can sink to the level of inferior beings. You can, if you so will, regenerate yourself in the likeness of superior beings.

The channeled teachings of Seth declare that, "We are gods couched in creaturehood." We are given the ability to form our experience and the Destiny we choose as our thoughts and feelings become actualized. Within the blueprint of each person's life lie many possibilities, alternations, and ramifications. Destiny is not a matter of chance or predetermination, it is a matter of choice. According to Seth, we can change the future.

At no time are events predestined. With every moment you change, and every action changes every other action.... You are not at the mercy of the subconscious, or helpless before forces that you cannot understand. The conscious mind directs unconscious activity and has at its command all of the power of the inner self. These are activated according to our ideas about reality.

Most psychics (see PSYCHIC/SENSITIVE) state that they cannot predict the absolute future because there are many *probable* destinies still in the making. They can only read their client's probable future based on the path the client has taken in the past and is following at present. Each thought you choose influences the destiny you will meet. As you expand in awareness, you learn to make better choices and can even alter your karma (see KARMA). You create your own reality, or we could say, *you create your own Destiny.*

Recommended Reading

Ashley, Nancy. *Create Your Own Reality: A Seth Workbook.* New York: Prentice-Hall, Inc., 1987. Places your destiny back in your own hands.

May, Rollo. *Freedom and Destiny.* New York: W. W. Norton, 1981. Insightful.

Plummer, George Winslow. *Consciously Creating Circumstances.* New York: Society of Rosicrucians, Inc., 1955.

Duality Theory

> *DUALITY THEORY states that the universe is composed of two opposing principles.*

Duality Theory is a belief in polarizing concepts such as right/wrong, mind/body, light/darkness, good/evil, spirit/matter, subject/object, winner/loser, heaven/hell, and so on. The illusion of Duality leads to greater separation from truth or Oneness (see UNITY/ONENESS). In Western civilization, God is portrayed as separate from man, unattainable, forever out of reach. Eastern religion, on the other hand, advocates non-Dualism with a belief in an underlying unity of all things.

In his book, *The Everything and the Nothing*, Avatar Meher Baba writes:

> *Duality implies separateness. Separateness causes fear. Fear makes worry. The way of Oneness is the way to happiness; the way of manyness is the way to worry.*

Left-brain intellectual analysis encourages Dualism by its very nature and widens the bridge between man and the Divine. The paradox is that man *is* simultaneously individual while also being one with the All That Is (see GOD/GODDESS/ALL THAT IS). This truth resides deep within the corridors of the collective mind and can only be comprehended intuitively. Our enchantment with Dualistic thought is explained in the channeled words of Emmanuel:

> *In your dualistic world there is great joy in dichotomy. It is part of the game of life you sometimes engage in that delights in pitting one side against the other in order to find a universal truth. This duality can, perhaps, serve the purpose of ultimate unification.... Those who are great thinkers have enjoyed for centuries separating the truth in order to dissect it. Then they forget the whole cloth they took it from...*

Recommended Reading

Briggs, John P., and F. David Peat. *Looking Glass Universe: The Emerging Science of Wholeness.* Santa Barbara, CA: Cornerstone Press, 1983.

Meher Baba. *The Everything and The Nothing.* Australia: Meher House Publications, 1963. Clarity to bridge Dualistic concepts.

Prigogine, Ilya, and Isabelle Stenger. *Order Out of Chaos.* New York: Bantam Books, 1984. Scientific search for order in the universe.

Forgiveness

> *FORGIVENESS is an act of healing, whether it is the outward Forgiveness of another or the inward Forgiveness of oneself.*

Unreleased feelings of rejection, resentment, hate, judgment, and guilt are damaging to ourselves and to others. Healing takes place when Forgiveness fills the heart. The process of Forgiving another person creates the simultaneous blessing of oneself — all other beings in the universe are but expressions of one's many aspects. Thomas Fuller once wrote, "He that cannot forgive others breaks the bridge over which he must pass himself..."

To Forgive someone for being limited is the loving act of dropping one's ego defenses and acknowledging one's own limitations and human misconceptions. Esoteric teachings (see ESOTERIC) advocate that through true understanding and the cleansing power of Forgiveness we reverse the Wheel of Karma (see KARMA). The dynamic power of Forgiveness creates a turning point toward a life of health, strength, happiness, and love. The following inspirations from *A Course in Miracles* reveal the courage and beauty held within Forgiveness:

> *You who want peace*
> *can find it only by forgiveness.*
> *Forgive the past and let it go,*
> *for it is gone.*
> *Lift up your eyes*
> *and look on one another in innocence*
> *born of complete forgiveness*
> *of each other's illusions.*

Recommended Reading

A Course in Miracles. Tiburon, CA: Foundation for Inner Peace, 1975. Perhaps the most well-known channeled works on psychological and spiritual development.

Finegold, Julius J., and William N. Thetford, editors. *Choose Once Again.* Berkeley: Celestial Arts, 1981. Selections from *A Course in Miracles.*

Jampolsky, Gerald, M.D. *Good-bye to Guilt.* New York: Bantam Books, 1988.

Jampolsky, Gerald, M.D. *Love is Letting Go of Fear.* New York: Bantam Books, 1985.

Shain, Merle. *Hearts That We Broke Long Ago.* New York: Bantam Books, 1983.

Singh, Tara. *Love Holds No Grievances.* Los Angeles: Life Action Press, 1988. Practical book which deals with healing relationships through Forgiveness and letting go of grievances.

Smedes, Lewis B. *Forgive and Forget: Healing the Hurts We Don't Deserve.* New York: Harper & Row, 1984.

Created
In His Own Image

God/Goddess/All That Is

God/Goddess/All That Is

> *GOD/GODDESS/ALL THAT IS refers to the infinite source of life.*

Most people feel there is a power greater than themselves. We witness the miracles that occur in our daily lives. Many feel guided by a divine force and grasp the idea that life is eternal. However or whatever words we use to describe our inner knowing of Infinite Love, it is with us always, it is "beyond words."

God/Goddess/All That Is is the term used by a channeled entity, Lazaris, to describe the divine awareness of Infinite Love. No matter what language we use, or which term we choose to call our infinite spirit...

> *We are the space where the IS dreams*
> *We are the imagination of the cosmos*
> *We are Infinite Love existing on*
> *visions and creativity...*

Alan Watts, author and visionary, tells a humorous story relating to God/Goddess/All That Is that goes this way:

> *God also likes to play hide-and-seek.... He pretends that he is you and I and all the people in the world, all the animals, all the plants, rocks and stars...*

> *Now when God plays hide-and-seek, and pretends that he is you and I, he does it so well that it takes him a long time to remember where and how he hid himself. But that's the whole fun of it —just what he wanted to do. He doesn't want to find himself too quickly, for that would spoil the game. That is why it is so difficult for you and me to find out that we are God in disguise, pretending not to be himself. But when the game has gone on long enough, all of us will wake up, stop pretending, and remember that we are all one single Self — the God who is all that there is and who lives for ever and ever.*

Recommended Reading

Literature of the great world masters: *The Bible; The Koran; The Upanishads & Vedas; Tao Te Ching; The Bhagavad Gita; The Torah.*

Christ, Carol P. *Laughter of Aphrodite: Reflection on a Journey to the Goddess.* Los Angeles: Harper & Row Publishers, 1987. The voice of the feminine.

Cole-Whittaker, Terry. *Love & Power in a World Without Limits: A Women's Guide to the Goddess Within.* New York: Harper & Row, 1989. Terry's newest insights.

Fynn. *Mister God This is Anna.* New York: Ballantine Books, 1974. A direct description of God/Goddess/All That Is as seen through the eyes of a young girl — a true story.

Haught, John. *What is God?* Mahwah, NJ: Paulist Press, 1986.

Lazaris. *The Sacred Journey: You and Your Higher Self.* Palm Beach, FL: NPN Publishing, Inc., 1987. A book from the originator of the term God/Goddess/All That Is.

Rifkin, Paul, editor. *The God Letters.* New York: Warner Books, Inc., 1986. Letters written by famous individuals in response to the question: Do you believe in God?

Smith, Houston. *The Religions of Man.* New York: Harper & Row, 1958.

Williams, Paul. *Remember Your Essence.* New York: Harmony Books, 1987. An inspirational meditation on the infinite source of life.

Higher-Self

> *The HIGHER-SELF is the pure Self at the very core of one's being. We are asleep to this Higher-Self except in rare moments of inspiration and illumination. It is the true center of consciousness that T.S. Eliot called the "still point of the turning world."*

Mystical belief and channeled literature contend that the lower-self we experience in day-to-day reality is but an illusion (see IL-LUSION/HOLOGRAM), a projection of the Higher-Self for the purpose of experiencing physical life on the Earth plane. It is believed that this Higher-Self is channeled downward to the lower-self through the *antahkarana* — *an umbilical-like connection.*

Ken Wilber, a leading figure in Transpersonal Psychology (see TRANSPERSONAL PSYCHOLOGY) and consciousness research, has stated his belief in a Higher Self, and that all of existence is a manifestation of that Self. This transpersonal Self, God-Self, Oversoul seems to exist in a timeless freedom beyond all separations. Intuition gives us a glimpse of the realm in which the Self lives. Illumination is said to bestow one with a complete view of that world and the experience of contacting it fully.

Three well-known authors discussed how they perceive their Higher-Self. Renowned psychotherapist Carl Jung believed that this universal-self or superconscious aspect of man is the origin of dreaming, the organizer and inventor. He theorized that it is this divine center of the psyche who sends images to the ego, necessary for personal growth and development. In his book, *Illusions*, Richard Bach writes, "You are led through your lifetimes by the inner learning creature, the playful spiritual being that is your real self." *Psychic Exploration,* edited by Edgar D. Mitchell describes the Higher-Self as working behind the scenes to guide the lower physical self:

> *Man, the perennial philosophy asserts, goes through life in a sort of hypnotic sleep, feeling that he is making decisions, having accidents occur to him, meeting chance acquaintances, and so on. If he begins to see more clearly... He becomes aware that decisions he felt he had come to logically or through intuition were really reflections of choices made on the higher*

*level of the self, that experiences and relationships that he
needed for his growth were attracted to him by the self and were
by no means so accidental as he had assumed.*

At present, the "skin-encapsulated ego" is the dominant model by
which our species perceives the world. As our consciousness evolves,
it is postulated that the individual ego — which has long been the center
of our inner universe — will assume its proper position, that of revolv-
ing around the true Self. Perhaps Ralph Waldo Emerson best captured
the divine essence of this Higher-Self and its influence in our lives in
his essay, "The Over-Soul:"

*When [the Higher-Self] breathes through [man's] intellect, it
is genius; when it breathes through his will, it is virtue; when
it flows through his affection, it is love.*

Recommended Reading

Lazaris. *The Sacred Journey: You and Your Higher Self.* Palm Beach,
FL: NPN Publishing, 1987.

Rengel, Peter. *Seeds of Light: Inspirations from My Higher Self.*
Tiburon, CA: H.J. Kramer, Inc., 1987. Read it, then buy a copy for
everyone you know.

Roberts, Jane. *The Education of Oversoul Seven.* New York: Prentice-Hall, Inc., 1973.

Roberts, Jane. *The Further Education of Oversoul Seven.* New York:
Prentice-Hall, Inc., 1979.

Roberts, Jane. *Oversoul Seven and the Museum of Time.* New York:
Prentice-Hall, Inc., 1984. A splendid trilogy, one was not enough!

Watts, Alan. *The Book: On the Taboo Against Knowing Who You Are.*
New York: Random House, Inc., 1972.

Williams, Paul. *Remember Your Essence.* New York: Harmony
Books, 1987. A special look at your Higher-Self.

Illusion/Hologram

ILLUSION means "not real." The realness of our universe, the material world, is but an Illusion. Quantum Theory reveals that our linear concepts of time and space are Illusional.

A HOLOGRAM is a "3-D" likeness of an image projected into space through laser technology. Unlike a normal photograph, a Hologram contains data about the entire image encoded in each point of the photographic plate. In other words, any point of the plate is capable of reproducing the entire Hologram. (Like a Hologram, the DNA of a human cell also contains all the genetic information needed to reproduce, or clone, the entire individual.)

What is reality and what is Illusion? Eastern religions advocate that all matter is an Illusion, or *maya* — a magic show. Prominent cyberneticist David Foster describes the Holographic quality of reality, by saying that we exist in "an intelligent universe whose apparent concreteness is generated by — in effect — cosmic data from an unknowable, organized source." He continues to say:

In a nutshell, the holographic super-theory says that our brains mathematically construct "hard" reality by interpreting frequencies from a dimension transcending time and space. The brain is a hologram, interpreting a hologram, interpreting a holographic universe. .

If we are living in some incredible Illusionary Holographic reality then this leads us to question: Who is running the Holographic projector? Who is out there looking in? Could this "organized source" be one's Higher-Self? (see HIGHER-SELF) Peter Rengel, author of *Seeds of Light: Inspirations from My Higher Self,* asks, "Aren't we humans so very fascinating? Who is creating this Miracle anyway?"

Modern physicists agree with the ancient mystics in calling the *stuff* of the world, "mind-stuff." At the subatomic level, science has found that the fabric of the universe may only be a Holographic pretense of the real — only vibrating energy patterns giving rise to the *appearance* of separate particles. David Bohm, a protégé of Einstein, said that what appears to be a stable, tangible, visible, audible world is an illusion — rather like watching a movie.

Then why does it all look and feel so real? It is suggested that if one were part of a Hologram, inside of it, everything else in the Hologram would appear real and solid. Only if one could step outside of the Hologram would its transparent quality and Illusional boundaries become evident. Psychologist and professor Keith Floyd has attempted to explain Holographic theory and human consciousness by saying:

> *It may not be the brain that produces consciousness — but rather, consciousness that creates the appearance of the brain —matter, space, time, and everything else we are pleased to interpret as the physical universe.*

Modern science, in answering fundamental inquiries about the nature of reality, has raised deeper questions which can only be answered intuitively. One such profound question asks: If the universe, and everything in it is a mirage, what then is the purpose of this grand Illusion? Mystics profess that God created the Illusion of physical reality for the learning adventure of experiencing the many aspects of Itself, through an eternal cosmic play.

Recommended Reading

Bach, Richard. *Illusions: The Adventures of a Reluctant Messiah.* New York: Dell Publishing Company, Inc., 1977. A brilliant best-seller, and that's not an Illusion.

Briggs, John P., and F. David Peat. *Looking Glass Universe: The Emerging Science of Wholeness.* Santa Barbara, CA: Cornerstone Press, 1983.

Capra, Fritjof. *The Tao of Physics.* New York: Bantam Books, 1976. A must for every library.

Herbert, Nick. *Quantum Reality: Beyond the New Physics.* New York: Doubleday, 1985. An excursion into metaphysics.

Wilber, Ken, editor. *The Holographic Paradigm and Other Paradoxes.* Boston: Shambhala Publications, 1988. Written for the lay reader by prominent scientists and thinkers.

Life Cycles

LIFE CYCLES commence approximately every seven years; therefore, each person periodically enters and travels through a new cycle or stage of life, incorporating past knowledge with new experiences, at around seven years old, 14 years, 21 years, 28 years, and so forth.

The seven year Life Cycle was first noted by Pythagoras and later discussed by Cicero and Seneca. All parts of an individual — physical, mental, and spiritual — require nourishment and replenishment to feed and restore the energy one expends in the course of life. According to astrologers we undergo a period of reenergizing to sustain the next seven year cycle. This renewal of energy replenishes and strengthens the total being. Patterns of beginning, transition and ending evolve in each seven year cycle.

In his book, *Cycles: The Mysterious Forces That Trigger Events,* Edward Dewey comments that if he were to investigate the possible connection between planetary cycles and earthly human cycles it would concern the electromagnetic forces of the universe. In astrology, this connection (whether electromagnetic, psychic, or other influences) is captured with the casting of the natal horoscope — each pie-shaped division corresponds to the twelve planets in a time-cycle of seven years.

Recommended Reading

Ballard, Juliet Brooke. *The Hidden Laws of Earth.* Virginia Beach, VA: A.R.E. Press, 1979. Based on the Edgar Cayce readings.

Dewey, Edward. *Cycles: The Mysterious Forces that Trigger Events.* Hudson, NY: Hawthorn Books, Inc., Div. of Anthroposophic Press, Inc., 1971. A complete book of universal and human cycles .

Manifestation

> *MANIFESTATION is the process of mind affecting outcome. Through the power of our conscious and subconscious desires, beliefs, feelings, imagination, and expectations, we manifest our physical reality.*

We are continuously manifesting. The life we are experiencing today is a product of the life we projected (consciously and unconsciously) for ourselves yesterday, last month, last year. Our choices and decisions return to haunt us or bestow us with rewards. In the book, *The Nature of Personal Reality,* Seth explains:

> *You are in physical existence to learn and understand that your energy, translated into feelings, thoughts and emotions, causes all experience. There are no exceptions.*

These universal laws of Manifestation can be used to our advantage. Once we realize we have the power to consciously manifest our experience, the fun begins! Through the use of techniques such as, visualization, affirmation, and working with the inner child (see RE-CREATION) we can unify our desires and expectations to *consciously* create our reality. Paying attention to our inner voices/whispers and keeping in touch with our intuition for guidance are ways of becoming more aware of the self-fulfilling prophecies (see SELF-FULFILLING PROPHECY) we are manifesting for our future.

Recommended Reading

Allen, James. *As a Man Thinketh.* New York: Grosset & Dunlap, 1984. A little book with *Big* ideas.

Anderson, U.S. *Three Magic Words.* North Hollywood, CA: Wilshire Book Company, 1954.

Ashley, Nancy. *Create Your Own Reality: A Seth Workbook.* New York: Prentice-Hall, Inc., 1987.

Cole-Whittaker, Terry. *How to Have More in a Have-Not World.* New York: Rawson Associates, 1983. Entertaining and instructive.

Harding, Khit. *Manifesting: A Master's Manual.* Eastbound, WA: Adam's Publishing Co., 1988. Steps for Manifesting.

Plummer, George Winslow. *Consciously Creating Circumstances.* New York: Society of Rosicrucians, Inc., 1955. Read it over and over.

Sher, Barbara, and Annie Gottlieb. *Wishcraft: How to Get What You Really Want.* New York: Ballantine Books, 1987.

Metaphysics

METAPHYSICS is a philosophy which speculates on, and questions, the nature of being.

The nature of being and beingness are concepts which have been questioned throughout time. As a noted teacher of philosophy says, "To know how to question means to know how to *wait*..." Humanity's existence, purpose, and meaning are poignant questions which have and will continue to be asked by metaphysicians. Metaphysical philosophy explores questions such as: What is the nature of being? Where do truth and reality converge? Is there such a thing as space or time? Why do I exist and what is death?

Like a child we ask questions to clear a path of knowledge for our unfolding-self. Questions like the ones above help us gather information needed for understanding ourselves, our world, and our universe. If all our questions could be answered, we would be able to hear an echo in the present. This is not possible, or is it? Our questioning minds (like a child's unending "whys?") must continue to reexamine the unanswerable. It is this examination which is accomplished within Metaphysics.

Edwin Burtt, author and philosopher, writes in his book, *The Metaphysical Foundations of Modern Science*, "...since human nature demands metaphysics for its full intellectual satisfaction, no great mind can wholly avoid playing with ultimate questions." Ultimate questions surrounding the basic problems of existence, the whys of the cosmos, are the blossoms on the tree of knowledge. Author and philosopher, Richard Taylor, writes, "It would probably be true to say that the fruit of metaphysical thought is not knowledge but understanding." Therefore, it is *understanding* of our cosmos, not mere knowledge, that becomes the true quest of Metaphysics.

Creation is not simply viewed as a continuum within Metaphysical thought, but as continuous. The universe is regarded as a whole body evolving — where the future is not only determined by the past and present, but also, the future affects that past and present through the timespace theories of simultaneous thought forms. This gives rise to the concept that our thoughts create reality — that *we create our own reality*. Spiritual teacher Krishnamurti agrees that thoughts create reality, but not necessarily truth. He writes, "Anything that we see, we see through our own experience, our own background. So that reality cannot possibly be totally independent of man[kind]." In other words, one can create one's own reality, but, because of held beliefs and values, one may never create truth.

Poet Edgar Allan Poe wrote of the reality dilemma: "Is all that we see or seem but a dream within a dream?" Potent questions like this one address the unseen realities of human nature. Metaphysics acknowledges that there is more to our universe than the mere physical material of the third dimension. It ponders the questions of "unseen" worlds of the fourth dimension. Reaching to heights of infinity, Metaphysics deals with topics like space, time, beingness, eternity, consciousness, spirit , ESP, and the nature of reality. Metaphysical concepts explore "beyond" the physical.

For an example, pain cannot be physically observed, but it can be Metaphysically perceived. It is beyond the physical eye's capability to see pain. What *is* observed are the effects of the pain, the distortions of the physical body and mind during the act of pain. So essentially, pain is a Metaphysical phenomenon. So too, we can say our spiritual nature is Metaphysical — that which lies beyond the physical boundaries of perception.

Based on quantum theory, transformation is the result of high energy sources grouping together to form a *new* idea, or reality. Richard Morris, author of *The Nature of Reality* feels many of the so-called "new" particles physicists have been discovering, are nothing more than *higher energy states of old ones*. This discovery of transformation is definitely a Metaphysical concept revealed in a physicist's laboratory. One cannot "see" the transformation happening, but it is a known occurrence. Taking this into consideration, one can understand the Metaphysical concept of spiritual transformation. In this New Age, higher energy states of consciousness throughout the globe are joining together to aid in spiritual evolution.

Richard Morris asks: "Is an understanding of the ultimate nature of physical reality something that is within the reach of the human mind?" He answers: "I simply feel that there is more to the universe than we are able to imagine." The unimaginable, "beyond pure reason," is exactly that which Metaphysics attempts to capture.

Perhaps tomorrow's metaphysics will begin as a critique
of science, just as in classical antiquity it began as a critique

of the gods. This metaphysics would ask itself the same questions as in classical philosophy, but the starting point of the interrogation would not be the traditional one before all science, but one after the sciences.

Octavio Paz, Latin American Surrealist Poet

Recommended Reading.

Burtt, Edwin. *The Metaphysical Foundations of Modern Science.* New York: Doubleday & Co., 1954.

de Chardin, Pierre Teilhard. *The Future of Man.* New York: Harper & Row, 1964. Tackles human nature and its future through science, philosophy, and theology.

Heidegger, Martin. *An Introduction to Metaphysics.* New Haven: Yale University Press, 1964. In-depth work in Metaphysics.

LeShan, Lawrence. *Alternate Realities.* New York: Ballantine Books, 1976. A study of the search for the full human.

Morris, Richard. *The Nature of Reality.* New York: McGraw-Hill Book Co., 1987. An eye-opening journey.

Pearce, Joseph Chilton. *The Crack in the Cosmic Egg.* New York: Julian Press, 1971.

Pearce, Joseph Chilton. *Exploring the Crack in the Cosmic Egg.* New York: Julian Press, 1974.

Smith, Huston. *Beyond the Post-Modern Man.* Rock Island, IL: Quest Publishing, 1982.

Taylor, Richard. *Metaphysics.* New York: Prentice-Hall, Inc., 1963. A good beginner in Metaphysics.

Young, Arthur. *The Bell Notes: A Journey from Physics to Metaphysics.* New York: Delacorte Press, 1984.

Microcosm/Macrocosm

A MICROCOSM is a smaller representative and aspect of a larger system (MACROCOSM).

Every Microcosm exists in relationship to a Macrocosm. The fashion in which each person behaves, relates, and thinks is said to be a reflection of the way in which our entire global culture behaves, relates and thinks. In other words, if one does not get along with one's next door neighbor, then that struggle is analogous to the wars of neighboring nations. Every Microcosm — whether it be a thought, an atom, or human being — is reflected and embodied in a Macrocosm.

Recommended Reading

Giono, Jean. *The Man Who Planted Trees*. Post Mills, VT: Chelsea Green Publishing, 1985. A delightful tale that illustrates how altruistic spirit can affect the world macrocosmically.

Harman, Willis. *Global Mind Change: The Promise of the Last Years of the Twentieth Century*. Indianapolis, IN: Knowledge Systems, Inc., 1988. Individuals can change their minds and macrocosmically affect change in the world.

Russell, Peter. *The Global Brain*. Los Angeles: J.P. Tarcher, Inc., 1983. Explores the connections between individual consciousness and the fate of the planet.

Mind Power

Mind Power

MIND POWER is the ability to control, or have power over the mind, the mind meaning both the conscious and subconscious.

We all like to think we have control over our own minds. How far from the truth this is depends upon our awareness, or the ability to perceive who we really are. How many of you reading this book really know who you are? Probably only a few could answer that they know. One of the reasons we cannot answer this question accurately is that we are *forever changing beings*; therefore, we are not this or that but ever-changing, ever-growing, ever-transforming. Why do we need to know who we are to learn about Mind Power? Simply put, if you do not know what your beliefs, values, patterns, ideals, or conditionings are — how could you begin to learn how to control them?

We have written herein how Mind Power over the *conscious* mind can relieve distress, pain, disease, and autonomic functions through autogenics, biofeedback, and self-hypnosis (see Individual Headings). Now we will look at how to control the *subconscious* mind's patterns, ideals, and blockages.

Studies have suggested that approximately 88 percent of your mind power is "subconscious" not "conscious." So to say you have Mind Power would be a mistake, unless you first investigated the realms of your subconscious mind. This is not to say that conscious Mind Power is not important, however, for this is where active manifestation begins (see MANIFESTATION).

To gain subconscious mind control one must begin at the beginning — one's birth. Imprinted upon the subconscious mind's computer is all the programing you have received from birth (actually before). By delving into your nature of consciousness, self-awareness, Higher-Self (see HIGHER-SELF) or whatever you desire to call it, the subconscious mind's patterns, ideals, desires, blockages, wishes and dreams, conflicts, likes and dislikes, and in essence every idea learned, experienced, or even witnessed, can be unlocked. With this releasing of "the you of you," doors open to the manifesting powers of your mind.

"The you of you" knows the subconscious mind and how to communicate with it. Using centering techniques such as meditation, prayers, chants and mantras, yoga, hypnosis, visualization, music or tonal resonance, and affirmations (see Individual Headings) one can touch the subconscious mind to unveil the true desires and the past programing which may be blocking their manifestation in the present.

Through detailed examination of your findings while searching the subconscious mind, allow all life's scripts to come before your consciousness. The power of your subconscious mind is tremendous and effort will be needed to resolve any conflicts of desires and patterns shown to you. To make total use of the power of your mind, it is necessary to align the conscious desires with the subconscious patterns. Begin with focusing on a current desire; a new car, a love relationship, career success. Look to the "you of you," the soul within, the subconscious awareness of who you are right now. Use one of the aforementioned techniques to guide you into a state of altered awareness (see ALTERED STATES OF CONSCIOUSNESS).

Upon your journey through the subconscious mind check any conflicts between what you experienced in the past and what you now hold as truth. Rectify these unresolved conflicts by actively, consciously, changing or re-creating it until the new form redefines your conscious knowledge and desire.

Take for example the desire for a new car. You have perhaps visualized this new car sitting in your driveway. You may have even gone so far as to affirm over and over that this is your desire. But alas, it has not arrived in your reality. Delving into your subconscious mind, you may find a childhood memory of your father telling you that you would "never amount to anything and would never own anything worthwhile." Can you imagine the conflict of interest between your conscious and subconscious minds? By reprogramming, or re-creating, your subconscious mind's experience to align with your conscious mind's desire, you can clear the blockage, and continue with the action of consciously creating your desire.

This may sound easy — it is! Joseph Murphy, author of *The Power of Your Subconscious Mind,* writes:

> *Many people block answers to their prayers by failing to fully comprehend the workings of their subconscious mind. When you know how your mind functions, you gain a measure of confidence. You must remember whenever your subconscious mind accepts an idea, (or experience) it immediately begins to*

execute it. It uses all its mighty resources to that end and mobilizes all the mental and spiritual laws of your deeper mind.

Recommended Reading

Anderson, U.S. *Magic Words.* North Hollywood, CA: Wilshire Book Co., 1976. Enlightening work on the mind's magic from a spiritual viewpoint.

Assagioli, Roberto. *The Act of Will.* New York: Penguin Books, 1987.

Maltz, Maxwell. *Psycho-Cybernetics & Self-Fulfillment.* New York: Grosset & Dunlap Publishers, 1970. A "how to" book.

Murphy, Joseph. *The Amazing Laws of Cosmic Mind Power.* Round Rock, TX: Parker Publishing Co., 1982. Incredible case histories prove how the power of the mind works miracles.

Murphy, Joseph. *The Power of Your Subconscious Mind.* New York: Bantam Books, 1982. Spell-binding philosophy of Mind Power.

Plummer, George Winslow. *Consciously Creating Circumstances.* New York: Society of Rosicrucians, Inc., 1983. Metaphysical dynamite found in a small booklet.

Science of Mind. Los Angeles: Science of Mind Publications and the United Church of Religious Science. A monthly magazine addressing the science of Mind Power.

Zdsnek, Marilee. *Inventing the Future.* New York: McGraw-Hill Book Co., 1987. Ways to help you alter your perception of yourself, therefore your future.

Miracles

MIRACLES are an expression of self love. They are the continual reminder of the Divine.

What is a miracle? Miracles are everywhere, happening every minute of existence. When we think of a miracle we usually embrace the process of birth, the healing of an illness, the luck of winning something of great value, or a prayer answered. Certainly each one of these acts *is* a miracle. However, how many of us also bring to awareness the act of breathing, the ocean's constant ebb and flow, or the never-ending cycles of the sun, earth, and moon? Miracles are a natural state of existence, an expression of love.

You might have noticed the bumper sticker which reads, "EXPECT A MIRACLE." Miracles happen when there is an attunement within and without. In the famous book, *A Course In Miracles*, it states that miracles are natural and when they do not occur something is wrong. Today it seems in order for a miracle to be accepted as such, an event must happen that is so *rare* that it "stands out from the ordinary." This is not the original meaning of the word. Miracles truly are found in abundance when one accepts love into one's life. As teacher and author, Terry Cole-Whittaker writes, "Love *gives* you everything and more than you ever dreamed of." The more you love yourself, the more you allow miracles to enter your life. "Someday mankind will learn that his horizon is not as he conceives it to be. He will learn that the horizon is limitless, and when man functions in a limitless world, it is then that every moment will be a miracle..."

Recommended Reading

A Course in Miracles. Tiburon, CA: Foundation for Inner Peace, 1984. Text and workbook to guide reader through miracles.

Gittner, Louis. *Listen - Listen - Listen.* Washington: The Louis Foundation, 1983. Opens the door to spiritual transformation.

Rodegast, Pat, and Judith Stanton. *Emmanuel's Book.* New York: Bantam Books, 1985. A manual full of miracles.

Siegel, Bernie S. *Love, Medicine & Miracles.* New York: Harper & Row, 1986. Long awaited work centering on the miracles of will and the use of the mind for healing.

Vaughan, Francis, and Roger Walsh, Editors. *Accept This Gift.* Los Angeles: J.P. Tarcher, Inc., 1983. Selection of writings from *A Course in Miracles.*

Prosperity/Abundance

> *PROSPERITY means success and is a state of mind. ABUNDANCE describes plenitude and is the result of choosing to live in a state of limitlessness over scarcity. Both terms may be manifested as an extension of the popular philosophy of positive thinking progressed to the understanding that one creates one's own reality.*

Poverty is an attitude based on one's belief system. It is thought that one's belief system resonates an energy that attracts or repels physical matter and circumstance. One continually creates life situations to support the negative or positive energy of one's beliefs. This innate power to create circumstance is explained in the book, *The Nature of Personal Reality*, by Jane Roberts:

> *Exterior events, circumstances and conditions are meant as a kind of living feedback. Altering the state of the psyche automatically alters the physical circumstances.... You change even the most permanent seeming conditions of your life constantly through the varying attitudes you have toward them. There is nothing in your exterior experience that did not originate within you.*

The area of Prosperity is often associated with material wealth which carries with it a lot of psychological baggage, much of it detrimental to achieving either Prosperity or Abundance. Society teaches confusing things about money, such as: spirituality and money do not mix; your friends, parents, or siblings will be jealous and you risk losing their love if you become more prosperous or successful than they; your ego will over inflate; you cannot have a successful career and a good love relationship, you must sacrifice one for the other, or; artists and writers must continually struggle.

For one who accepts the fallacy that money is evil or hard to come by, it will be. For one who believes there is a limit to wealth and not enough to go around, there won't be. But for those who believe they can achieve Prosperity and Abundance, who visualize that achievement, and who consciously act in a way to inspire and encourage it — the sky's the limit. This is the wisdom behind tithing, or giving to charity, or donating one's time and talents. The act of giving says, in effect, there is plenty of this to go around; I am not afraid of being without; this gift, this gesture, re-affirms my belief in the universal abundant flow.

Recommended Reading

Cole-Whittaker, Terry. *How to Have More in a Have-Not World.* New York: Rawson Associates, 1983. Basic, instructive, and rewarding.

Ponder, Catherine. *Open Your Mind to Prosperity.* Unity Village, MO: Unity Books, 1971. A must for every metaphysical library.

Ponder, Catherine. *The Dynamic Laws of Prosperity.* New York: Prentice-Hall, Inc., 1962.

Roman, Sanaya, and Duane Packer. *Creating Money.* Tiburon, CA: H.J. Kramer, Inc., 1987. Keys to Abundance.

Sinetar, Marsha. *Do What You Love, The Money Will Follow.* New York: Paulist Press, 1987.

Taylor, Holland. *The Prosperity Book.* Michael Fries & Co. Communications Research, 1984. A practical overview of Prosperity in today's society.

Psychosynthesis

> *PSYCHOSYNTHESIS is a type of therapy which encourages and promotes positive psychological and spiritual growth based on learning how to handle emotions in the here and now.*

Roberto Assagioli, an Italian psychiatrist, developed the term Psychosynthesis while constructing a new method of psychoanalytic thought. Defining Psychosynthesis, we find "psycho," a Greek word meaning the soul, spirit, or mind; and the word "synthesis," to combine various parts to form a whole. Thus, Psychosynthesis emerges as a system of therapy directed to combining or joining the many parts of the mind to form a whole, healthy, functioning individual.

Some of the areas touched upon by Psychosynthesis are the development of the will; transmutation of sexual and aggressive drives; the awareness of (and responsibility for) decisions and choices; and the recognition of the positive, creative, and joyful experiences in one's life. Through the numerous techniques used in Psychosynthesis, an individual is educated in how to focus on the present and the feelings it brings to the conscious mind. The current emotional blocks are reshaped to unfold a healthy enjoyable life.

Recommended Reading

Assagioli, Roberto. *The Act of Will.* New York: Penguin Books, 1987. One of the original works.

Assagioli, Roberto. *Psychosnythesis.* New York: Penguin Books, 1986. Technical explanation for professionals.

Brown, Molly Young. *The Unfolding Self: Psychosynthesis and Counseling.* San Francisco: Psychosynthesis Press, 1983. A workbook for discovering the Self.

Ferrucci, Piero. *What We May Be: Techniques for Psychological and Spiritual Growth.* Los Angeles: J.P. Tarcher, Inc., 1982. A well rounded and detailed account of the process of Psychosynthesis.

The Psychosynthesis Institute can be contacted by writing to: 3352 Sacramento Street, San Francisco, CA 94117.

Quantum Physics

> QUANTUM PHYSICS is the science of atomic and
> subatomic particles, the building blocks of the
> universe.

When asked about the dynamics of the Uncertainty Principle,
renowned physicist Sir Arthur Eddington replied, "Something unknown
is doing we don't know what." Likewise, Werner Heisenberg, one of
the scientists responsible for formulating quantum mechanics, once
wrote, "anyone who is not shocked by quantum theory does not understand it." What is there to be shocked about? Physicists have come to
realize that they cannot merely _observe_ an experiment as outsiders; their
results are dependent on what they _expect_ to find. In other words, on
subatomic levels, we create with our thoughts and expectations that
which will come to pass.

Another discovery of Quantum Theory implies that what our brains
register as "real" is actually an illusion (see ILLUSION/HOLOGRAM)
created by our "neurologically primitive perceptual system." Evidently
atoms and subatomic units lend _apparent_ reality to temporary, radiant,
interconnected, eternally-in-motion living energy. This energy is sta-
tioned within a boundary that we identify as a chair, another person, and
all other physical matter. These recent findings in Quantum Physics are
astonishing even to the scientists conducting the experiments.
Physicists such as Fritjof Capra are beginning to see our universe from
an entirely new perspective:

> The universe is no longer seen as a machine, made up of a
> multitude of objects, but it has to be pictured as one indivisible,
> dynamic whole whose parts are essentially interrelated and can
> be understood only as patterns of cosmic process.

Another startling idea in Quantum Physics has been theorized by
French physicist Jean Charon. In his book, _The Unknown Spirit_,
Charon maintains that electrons, the most numerous particles in the
universe — almost a hundred billion in each cell of our bodies and our
bodies contain billions of cells — are the missing link between the
spiritual world and what we perceive as the physical universe. Quantum Physics identifies electrons as points without measurable mass, yet

science acknowledges that they must take up space somewhere. Charon compares the electron to a mini black hole and contends that it exists in a spacetime (see TIME/SPACE) which touches ours only at a single point.

These elementary particles have existed since the dawn of time and are the fabric of the universe. They live forever, remember every experience, and communicate with all other electrons in the universe. Charon reflects that this may explain the phenomenon of past life memory. He also believes that electrons think, learn, love, store and review information, and respond to the world around them. While science continues to look for proof of mind and spirit amid flesh and bones, Charon holds that we will one day see the electron as the doorway into the spiritual dimension for which we have long searched.

The world's greatest physicists — Pauli, Planck, Jeans, Heisenberg, Schroedinger, de Broglie, Eddington, and Einstein — have all come to hold that mysticism and physics are in essence fraternal twins. Current high-energy physicists continue to use words and phrases similar to those used by the ancient mystics to describe the transcendental workings of the universe. Peter Russell, author of *The Global Brain*, points out:

> *Even though these theories are coming from physicists, they are beginning to sound more and more like the teachings of the mystics.... The physicist is probing the deepest levels of objective existence using the tools of physical experimentation, reason, and mathematics, whereas the mystic is probing the deepest levels of subjective existence through personal introspection.*

Recommended Reading

Capra, Fritjof. *The Tao of Physics*. New York: Bantam Books, 1975. Will science lead us to the Buddha or the Bomb?

Davies, Paul. *God and the New Physics*. New York: Simon & Schuster, Inc., 1983.

Kaku, Michio, and Jennifer Trainer. *Beyond Einstein*. New York: Bantam Books, 1987. Easy to read, non-technical overview of physics.

Nucleus, a quarterly publication of the Union of Concerned Scientists. A nonprofit organization of scientists and other citizens concerned with the impact of advanced technology on the world.

Wilber, Ken, editor. *Quantum Questions*. Boston: New Science Library, 1984. Mystical writings of the world's great physicists.

Wolf, F.A. *Taking the Quantum Leap: The New Physics for Nonscientists*. New York: Harper & Row, 1981. Mind-expanding clarity for the layman.

Re-Creation

Re-Creation

RE-CREATION© is a transforming process of reaching, touching, and accepting the inner child; the process continues with a releasing of blockages and re-creating past emotional trauma to re-form the creative vital force found within the adult.

The Process of Re-creation is based on, and is an expansion of, the concept of the *inner child* which resides within each of us. When we became adults we put away our "child within" believing that our childhood was over and the past no longer mattered. However, this child within still plays, laughs, cries, yells, and even stomps when upset. The inner child is also loving, caring, and compassionate. Through the various counseling techniques of Re-Creation, one can begin to understand the fears, self-imposed limits, desires, and beliefs which were accepted as a child but no longer serve the adult nature.

We are a product of all that we have heard, seen, and felt. Through Re-Creation, our inner child becomes a messenger carrying information regarding the origin of our present beliefs, values, and motivations. This process gives us the tools to release our intrinsic power to create the circumstances, abundance and love we wish to experience in our present reality.

The past is but a memory locked within the subconscious mind. Through the Process of Re-Creation we learn there are no time barriers and through the use of Hypnotherapy and creative Visualization (see HYPNOSIS/HYPNOTHERAPY AND VISUALIZATION) we can create a positive present by re-creating the past. Our present experiences are influenced by past memories contained in our subconscious mind. When we change the emotional remembrance of these events, we also change our current attitudes, beliefs, and motivations toward our present reality.

We can manifest a creative and successful present and future by re-programing the past stored in our subconscious minds. As a child we could not choose the belief structure or conditioning we received from our parents, peers, and environment. As an adults, we *can* re-program or re-write our past scripts, the roles being played in the present. Re-Creation is a dynamic therapy process which works simply and gently to help one manifest a limitless future.

Recommended Reading

Sinor, Barbara, M.A., CHT, and Paula Slater, M.A., CHT. *Gifts From the Child Within.* A therapy reference book now in progress. It introduces the Process of Re-Creation.[©]

Self-Fulfilling Prophecy

> *A SELF-FULFILLING PROPHECY is the process by which a person's expectations are brought into fulfillment through their thoughts and actions. Even if we are unaware of the connection between our thoughts and their manifestation, Self-Fulfilling Prophecies are proof of the power we possess to create our own reality.*

The expectations we hold today will become the Self-Fulfilled Prophecy we experience tomorrow. In James Allen's book, *As a Man Thinketh*, he states, "The outer world of circumstance shapes itself to the inner world of thought..." Thought creates circumstance; there is no escaping this universal law.

We can use our marvelous mind power (see MIND POWER) to our advantage by projecting Self-Fulfilling Prophecies we would like to experience in our lives. It is more fun to celebrate the benefits of positive thought-projections, but too often we claim, "I just knew it was too good to be true," when our negative thought-projections tumble back on us.

In this New Age, growing numbers of people are awakening to the realization that some things have to be *believed* to be *seen*. Thus, we must take full responsibility for the innate power of our thoughts and expectations in order to improve the quality of our lives and of life on Earth.

Recommended Reading

Allen, James. *As a Man Thinketh*. New York: Grosset & Dunlap, 1984.

Anderson, U.S. *Three Magic Words*. North Hollywood, CA: Wilshire Book Company, 1954. A valued friend.

Ashley, Nancy. *Create Your Own Reality: A Seth Work-book*. New York: Prentice-Hall, Inc., 1987. To be studied in detail, and then *lived*.

Plummer, George Winslow. *Consciously Creating Circumstances*. New York: Society of Rosicrucians, Inc., 1955. This little book is "full of metaphysical dynamite."

Self-Love/Self-Worth

SELF-LOVE and SELF-WORTH are aspects of human nature which can be attained and transformed.

Self-Love follows self-awareness and self-acceptance. In order to fully love yourself unconditionally (see UNCONDITIONAL LOVE), there must be a total recognition, an *awareness* of who you are "inside and out." *Self-acceptance* then follows *self-awareness*. One can be *aware* of their total being (mind, body, and spirit) but still not *accept* or feel positive about what is found. Arriving at a state of self-acceptance takes time, self-observation, and introspection.

Author Susan Page believes Self-Love is not about loving the parts of yourself that are easy to love because there is no challenge in this; rather Self-Love is loving *all* yourself, including the parts you do not like or may not wish to look at or acknowledge. Self-awareness, self-acceptance, and Self-Love can lead one to the process of changing or Re-creating (see RE-CREATION) those parts that no longer appeal to you.

Self-Love is the gift you receive if you dare to challenge your "whole-self" to reveal painful aspects hidden in your subconscious mind. You cannot *will* this to happen. The gift of Self-Love must be unwrapped slowly and gently, allowing the bows, ribbons, and layers of paper-selves to fall away — only then can true Self-Love emerge to expose the total human-self.

Self-Worth can be maintained, even in times of fluctuation, with a firm foundation of Self-Love to guide you. Self-Worth (or self-esteem) is developed in the early childhood years and, sadly, low self-esteem is many times extended into adult lives. Self-Worth tends to be associated with "some thing or aspect" of ourselves, i.e., intelligence, money, family, fame, and so on. Self-Worth has nothing to do with one's "accomplishments." It is not about who you are or what you have. It is about how you *feel* about who you are and what you have.

Also, Self-Worth is usually associated with an "outer-directed" event, experience, or person. To maintain a healthy, positive feeling of Self-Worth, one must look *within* and also become an "inner-directed" person allowing the gift of Self-Love to reside deep within. One can reveal the treasure of the true relationship with oneself.

Recommended Reading

Hay, Louise. *You Can Heal Your Life.* Santa Monica, CA: Hay House, 1984. A look at the nature of completing the cycle of Self-Loving through healing.

Hillig, Chuck. *The Magic King.* Walpole, NH: Stillpoint Publishing, 1984. A children's book about a magical king who teaches that "love is the secret of his power."

Jampolsky, Gerald. *Love is Letting Go of Fear.* Berkeley: Celestial Arts, 1979.

Kraft-Macoy, Liah. *30 Days to Happiness: Setting Yourself Up to Win in Life.* Walpole, NH: Stillpoint Publishing, 1987. Developing Self-Worth on a daily basis.

Ray, Sondra. *I Deserve Love.* Berkeley: Celestial Arts, 1987. Small but powerful book on loving yourself.

Satir, Virginia. *Self-Esteem.* Berkeley: Celestial Arts, 1972 Short and light to lift the spirit.

Satir, Virginia. *People Making.* Palo Alto, CA: Science & Behavior Books, Inc., 1975. An instruction to attaining total wholeness.

Subliminal

> *SUBLIMINAL perception is an unconscious response to stimuli that are below the threshold of conscious awareness.*

In the 1950's, Subliminal stimulation was the subject of heated controversy. A New Jersey movie theater flashed Subliminal messages on the screen during the showing of a movie appropriately called *Picnic*. Unbeknown to its patrons, Subliminal messages such as "Drink Coca-Cola®," and "Hungry? Eat popcorn," were flashed across the screen every five seconds. There were claims of increased popcorn and Coke® sales. This technique has since been subject to governmental regulation to protect the public.

Subliminals work by bypassing the normal censors of the conscious mind. It is believed if you strengthen the subconscious acceptance of an idea, your conscious will power is then strengthened as well. The question of ethics has been raised in conjunction with Subliminals because of the opportunity for abusing this technology. The dark side of Subliminal stimulation could be the use of "persuasion machines" for brainwashing by slipping messages past the conscious mind into the subconscious in less than three-thousandths of a second. However, one can utilize this technology to "sneak" positive messages into the subconscious, hence altering one's negative or outmoded beliefs.

Subliminal reprogramming has been promoted as "effortless self-improvement," "twilight learning," and "subliminal psychodynamic activation." Through the use of subliminals it is said that one can strengthen will power and modify addictive behavior. This method has been used to lessen stress, inhibit psychosomatic pain, diminish procrastination, reduce phobias, alleviate alcohol and drug problems, stop smoking, lose weight, increase self-esteem and confidence, overcome shyness and fear of public speaking; and just about any other woe of humankind. As with affirmations (see AFFIRMATION), it is recommended that Subliminal messages be short, sweet, and positive.

Subliminal messages can be hidden in audio cassettes, videotapes, even wallpaper and writing paper can "whisper to the eye." For the avid computer user, Subliminal software packages are presently available. While hacking away at the computer you can punch in any message you want to feed your subconscious mind. Every one-thirtieth of a second your Subliminal communique will invisibly flash across the top of your computer screen — an eight-hour day equals 30,000 affirmative flashes. Now, that's user-friendly!

Recommended Reading

Key, Wilson Bryan. *Subliminal Seduction.* New York: New American Library, 1974.

Myers, Frederic W. *Subliminal Consciousness.* Salem, N H: Ayer Publishers, Inc., 1976.

Subliminal Suggestions, a computer software program available through: New Life Institute, P.O. Box 2390, Santa Cruz, CA 95063. (408) 429-1122.

Synchronicity

> *SYNCHRONICITY is considered to be any meaningful coincidence of two or more events where something other than the probability of chance is involved.*

Synchronicity cannot be scientifically validated like other psychic phenomena. Synchronistic events are those which defy our scientific knowledge, as yet. Russell Targ, author of *The Mind Race*, believes Synchronistic events are most likely examples of acausally related happenings. This means there is no explanation of how or why these events happen when they do; there is no *cause* or reason for their happening, and at the same time, they are not causally connected.

Synchronistic, or simultaneous events which seem to happen by coincidence are experienced by all of us — as if there were a higher power controlling an unfolding picture of a puzzle. Synchronistic events are coincidences which cannot be ignored, for they open our eyes to the "larger picture" of reality and our ears to the "whispers of guidance" (see INNER VOICES/WHISPERS).

Recommended Reading

Bolen, Jean Shinoda, M.D. *The Tao of Psychology: Synchronicity and the Self.* New York: Harper & Row, 1979.

Jung, C.G. *The Structure & Dynamics of the Psyche-Synchronicity: An Acausal Connecting Principle.* New York: New York University Press, 1973. Original works by person coining the term.

Peat, F. David. *Synchronicity: The Bridge Between Matter and Mind.* New York: Bantam Books, 1987. Do coincidences reflect the relationship between matter and mind?

Progoff, Ira. *Jung, Synchronicity, and Human Destiny.* New York: The Julian Press, 1973.

Vaughan, Alan. *Incredible Coincidences.* New York: Lippincott, 1979. A collection of Synchronistic events.

Von Franz, Marie-Louise. *On Divination & Synchronicity: The Psychology of Meaningful Chance.* Canada: Inner City Books, 1980.

Time/Space

Time/Space

TIME/SPACE is a never ending evolution of change.

To speak of time one must first talk of Beingness, which is derived from the conscious mind — it is eternity's consciousness. This Beingness is in constant evolution, always growing and transforming. Beingness occupies no space — eternity's consciousness *Is*. Beingness has no time — there are no limits to eternity.

"There is no time, only change" it has been written. If there is only change, and change is never ending, then time becomes a never ending succession of changes occurring infinitely. There is then, no past or future, only the ever changing present. The authors of *Space, Time & Beyond* said it this way, "The past and the future are both rolled up in this present moment of illumination, and this present moment is not something standing still with all its contents, for it ceaselessly moves on."

Einstein's theory of relativity shows us that Space is not three dimensional, and Time is not a separate entity. Both are intimately connected and form a four-dimensional continuum, a TimeSpace. This TimeSpace continuum exists within our Beingness — eternity's consciousness. TimeSpace *is* the Eternal Now.

To take this even one step further — the Eternal Now is existing as the totality of all pasts, presents, and futures. In other words, all time is simultaneous — our Beingness is manifesting concurrently. This truth may be rather difficult to comprehend; however, it has been established both metaphysically and scientifically. The channeled entity, Seth, put it this way:

> *There simply is no time as you think of it, only a present in which all things occur.... Space itself accelerates in ways that you do not understand. You are not tuned into those frequencies. Any point in space is also a point in what you think of as time, a doorway that you have not learned to open.*

Beingness is TimeSpace. There is no past, present, or future — only illusion (see ILLUSION/HOLOGRAM). Everything in the universe exists at one time; even our *past* lives (see REINCARNA-TION) are happening concurrently! There is a grander scope of Time and Space which our vision has yet to see; for all time's secret treasures lie in eternity.

Recommended Reading

Bach, Richard. *Illusions.* New York: Dell Publishing, 1977.

Bach, Richard. *One.* New York: William Morrow & Co., 1988

Capra, Fritjof. *The Tao of Physics.* New York: Bantam Books, 1984. Qualitative and factual.

Houston, Jean. *The Possible Human: A Course in Extending Your Physical, Mental & Creative Abilities.* Los Angeles: J.P. Tarcher, 1982. Exercises dealing with TimeSpace.

LeShan, Lawrence, and Henry Margenau. *Einstein's Space & Van Gogh's Sky: Physical Reality and Beyond.* New York: Macmillan, 1982. In-depth overview.

Morris, Richard. *Time's Arrows: Scientific Attitudes Toward Time.* New York: Simon & Schuster, Inc., 1986. Filled with intriguing questions.

Roberts, Jane. *The Seth Material.* New York: Prentice-Hall, Inc., 1970. Channeled information regarding reality and illusion.

Tarthang Tulku. *Time, Space, & Knowledge: A New Vision of Reality.* Berkeley, CA: Dharma Publishing, 1977. Exercises for exploring other dimensions.

Toben, Robert, and Fred Wolf. *Space, Time & Beyond.* New York: Bantam Books, 1983. Paperback with cartoons to help understand the concept.

Transpersonal Psychology

TRANSPERSONAL PSYCHOLOGY is an approach to healing which integrates mind, body, and spirit.

Transpersonal Psychology is an emerging division of psychology which addresses the study of human nature. It encompasses not only the three major branches of psychology — Psychoanalytic theory; Behaviorism; and the Humanistic approach — but also attempts to capture the ever-changing, or transformative aspects of human growth patterns.

The word Transpersonal has two parts, "trans" meaning across, beyond, or to change completely; and "personal," pertaining to the personal, or personality. Transpersonal is defined as beyond the person, or to change and reach across the personal awareness and individual ego. This interpretation fosters the ability to grasp the total personhood (mind, body, and spiritual nature) to reach beyond our familiar level of ego awareness to a critical examination of behaviors, thoughts, and emotions which spur *conscious transformation.*

Ralph Metzner, Academic Dean at the California Institute of Integral Studies, defines consciousness as "the context, or field, in which thoughts, feelings, perceptions, sensations, images, impulses, intentions...exist and occur." With this definition of consciousness we can say "conscious transformation" occurs when any of the following transpire: changes in thinking regarding world views, beliefs, goals; changes in the feelings that surround motives, values, love, compassion and support; changes in perception such as ESP or spiritual awareness experiences. When changes such as these occur it can be called *conscious self-transformation.* These conscious transformations are the building blocks of Transpersonal counseling.

The ultimate goal of Transpersonal counseling is to guide one through the act of conscious self-transformation to a state of trust, faith, acceptance of self and others, and to generate self-esteem and self-love (see SELF-LOVE/SELF-WORTH). Carl Jung's term, individuation, meaning to become a separate individual and "in-divisible" or whole, also describes what Transpersonal counseling strives to accomplish. Guiding another toward attaining a sense of conscious awareness and individual transformation becomes the cornerstone of Transpersonal Psychology.

Recommended Reading

Grof, Stanislav, editor. *Human Survival and Consciousness Evolution.* New York: SUNY Press, 1988. A compilation of noted authorities in the field.

Metzner, Ralph. *Opening to Inner Light: The Transformation of Human Nature & Consciousness.* Los Angeles: J.P. Tarcher, Inc., 1986.

Tart, Charles C. *Transpersonal Psychologies.* New York: Harper & Row, 1975. In-depth review.

Vaughan, Francis. *The Inward Arc.* Boston: Shambhala, 1986. A Transpersonal Psychotherapist discusses human development clarifying the physical, emotional, mental, existential, and spiritual natures needed for optimum health.

Walsh, Roger, and Francis Vaughan, editors. *Beyond Ego: Transpersonal Dimensions in Psychology.* Los Angeles: J.P. Tarcher, Inc., 1980.

Wilber, Kenneth. *The Atman Project: A Transpersonal View of Human Development.* Wheaton, IL: The Theosophical Publishing House, 1980. A thorough look at developmental psychologies.

Universal Laws/Principles

> *UNIVERSAL LAWS or PRINCIPLES govern our ex-
> istence and the order of the cosmos. We are in har-
> mony with the universe when we act in accordance
> with these spiritual laws.*

As we expand our consciousness, we become aware of certain
principles that when followed bring order to our lives. These eternal
laws are in continual operation whether we are aware of them or not.
They form the vital, yet sensitive, structure in which the cosmos is held.
Among these spiritual principles are unity, balance, order, proportion,
and rhythm. These laws are observed as composing the very foundations of nature. Lyall Watson, author of *Lifetide*, states that to *disbelieve*
in the existence of these organizing cosmic principles "is tantamount to
assuming that the Encyclopaedia Britannica was thrown together by an
explosion in a printing works."

Philosophers, spiritual teachers, and poets have long known that
these Universal Principles prevail. One such law dictates that for every
physical occurrence there is a corresponding metaphysical (see
METAPHYSICS) reason or cause. This is the universal law of karma
(see KARMA) or the law of "cause and effect." Another cosmic
principle states, "That which you truly accept shall be yours." A basic
metaphysical law declares that "matter follows thought." A universal
rule that is all too familiar reads, "The only constant, is change."

Universal Laws have been articulated by gifted people down
through the ages. Avatar Meher Baba gave voice to the powerful truth
that the only *Real Existence* is that of the one and only God who is the
Self. Through the channeled writings of *A Course in Miracles*, we
learn, "What you perceive in others you are strengthening in yourself."
Poet and philosopher Kahlil Gibran intuited this spiritual law:

> *And as a single leaf turns not yellow but
>   with the silent knowledge of the whole tree,
> So the wrong-doer cannot do wrong
>   without the hidden will of you all.
> Like a procession you walk together
>   towards your god-self.*

Recommended Reading

Gibran, Kahlil. *The Prophet.* New York: Alfred A. Knopf, Inc., 1973. A masterpiece of universal principles.

Meher Baba. *The Everything and the Nothing.* Australia: Meher House, 1963. Principles that breathe order into the universe.

Rodegast, Pat, and Judith Stanton, editors. *Emmanuel's Book.* New York: Bantam Books, 1987. Living comfortably within cosmic law.

Rodegast, Pat, and Judith Stanton, editors. *Emmanuel's Book II — The Choice for Love.* New York: Bantam Books, 1989.

Yin/Yang, Anima/Animus

Yin/Yang, Anima/Animus

> *YIN/YANG are terms found in Eastern philosophy denoting the archetypal poles of cyclic change within nature.*

> *ANIMA/ANIMUS are terms coined by C.G. Jung to address the opposite, but at the same time, balance between a person's feminine and masculine qualities.*

Yin refers to the dark, receptive, female qualities; Yang is the light, creative, male power. These two concepts comprise the natural flow of life, both within and without. As the Chinese philosopher Chuang Tzu once said, "Life is the blended harmony of the yin and yang." The harmonic patterns within all nature (including humankind) are portrayed in the symbology of the Yin/Yang principle.

In Chinese medicine such as acupuncture (see ACUPUNC-TURE/ACUPRESSURE) the balance of Yin/Yang energy within the body is necessary for optimum health. The body and organs are divided into Yin/Yang parts which must have a continuous flow of energy, or chi, along certain meridians to maintain balance and wholeness. Also, the ancient Chinese *I Ching* (see I CHING) is based on the Yin/Yang principle of change.

Carl Jung introduced the Anima/Animus theory to guide our understanding of the balancing natures of personality. He takes the principles of the Chinese Yin/Yang philosophy to the soul level within man/woman. Jung denotes that in the unconscious of every man there is a hidden feminine personality and in that of every woman a hidden masculine. This feminine within man, Jung calls the Anima; the masculine within woman is the Animus.

The Anima/Animus concept is analogous to the Chinese Yin/Yang principle. Within each male and each female there are both propensities — the lesser sex energy lying somewhat dormant. The challenge is to balance these two opposites to create an inner and outer harmony of masculine and feminine; to allow the active forces of male energy (animus/yang) to blend with the inspirational aspects of our feminine nature (anima/yin).

Recommended Reading

Capra, Fritjof. *The Tao of Physics*. New York: Bantam Books, 1984. Brief overview of Yin/Yang principles.

Hillman, James. *Anima: An Anatomy of a Personified Notion*. Dallas, TX: Spring Publications, Inc., 1985. Quotes by Carl Jung.

Jung, Carl, *The Essential Jung*, "The Syzygy: Anima and Animus," Princeton, NJ: Princeton University Press, 1983.

Jung, Emma. *Animus & Anima*. Dallas TX: Spring Publications, Inc., 1987. Classic essays on the archetypal psyche.

The Psychic Window

"Don, walking through walls, it isn't hard for me now; it is impossible."

"Do you think that maybe if you say impossible over and over again a thousand times that suddenly hard things will come easy for you?... Argue for your limitations and you get to keep them," he sang.

Richard Bach, *Illusions*

Altered States of Consciousness (ASC)

> *ALTERED STATES OF CONSCIOUSNESS are states of consciousness that are qualitatively different from one's ordinary waking state of mind.*

Classically, we have called limited, ordinary, waking awareness our "normal" state of consciousness. All other levels of awareness, we refer to as an *Altered State of Consciousness.* Studies have been performed to measure brain wave activity recorded on an EEG to determine levels of consciousness: A few cycles per second (hertz) indicates an individual in deep delta-wave sleep; an increase to a few more hertz signals theta states associated with creativity, learning, and reverie. Alpha-waves reflecting relaxation and meditation begin around seven to twelve hertz. Eighteen to thirty hertz denotes the beta-wave "chatter" of the waking state, with its analytical processing and environmental interaction.

Jack Schwartz, a researcher in psychoenergetic states, has personally experienced "hyperaesthetic" states of consciousness which allow him to reach into paranormal and transcendent levels. Others have delighted in "introverted mystical experiences" (unity without sensory activity) and "extroverted mystical experiences" (a sensory level of body-earth knowing). Through drug experimentation or devoting much of their lives to rigorous and lengthy disciplines, many people have attempted to experience these rewarding altered states.

Eastern meditation techniques have been used by artists in Tibet, India, and Japan throughout history to achieve a relaxed state of awareness to stimulate the creative centers of the mind. Dreaming and half-dreaming states can produce a wide array of symbolic images and fantasies which are the language of the unconscious mind. Although Altered States of Consciousness can be induced through various means, most of us slip in and out of these expanded levels of awareness without even knowing it.

Recommended Reading

Pelletier, Kenneth. *Toward a Science of Consciousness.* New York: Dell Publishing Co., 1978.

Tart, Charles T. *States of Consciousness and Altered States of Consciousness.* New York: E.P. Dutton & Co., 1963; and North Carolina: UMI Publications, Inc., 1969. Informational.

Taylor, Eugene, editor. *William James on Exceptional Mental States.* Amherst: University of Massachusetts Press, 1982. Reconstruction of 1896 Lowell Lectures of William James.

Apparition/Ghost/Poltergeist

An APPARITION is the appearance of the non-material essence of an organism; human or nonhuman and objects which interact with the viewer.

A GHOST is the nonmaterial essence of a human which can or cannot interact with the viewer.

A POLTERGEIST refers to a type of disturbance in which recurrent spontaneous psychokinesis is observed.

Apparitions can be broken into four main categories: (1) apparitions of the living, (2) crisis apparitions, (3) post-mortem apparitions, and (4) continual apparitions or ghosts. The term "haunting" refers to a location or sighting of where an Apparition is observed.

Apparitions of the living occur when one uses the inner vision of the psychic mind and "envisions" another person. This can happen during an OBE (see OUT-OF-BODY EXPERIENCE) or in an altered state of consciousness during relaxation (see ALTERED STATES OF CONSCIOUSNESS). An example would be when someone close to you is away for a trip and you sense their presence near you, perhaps to the point of actually visually seeing their form as a misty-type figure.

Crisis Apparitions are not classified as either living or dead. Apparitions of this category form a large percentage of the reports by people who experience a visitation from someone known to them, either living or dead. Noted parapsychologist and author, D. Scott Rogo, has beliefs as to the origin of such Crisis Apparitions. His hypothesis is that we are not actually seeing them with our eyes but perhaps the apparition, appearing in some sort of fourth dimension, is rather igniting our clairvoyance (see CLAIRVOYANCE/CLAIRAUDIENCE). With this interpretation, an Apparition becomes linked with its percipient psychically. This would explain the phenomenon of only a select group of individuals reporting Ghosts or Apparitions when in a room filled with people.

An example of a crisis Apparition would be when a person sees with their "third eye" (see THIRD EYE) an image of another person in distress. One such instance occurred to a young mother while her seven-year-old boy, Billy, was playing in a field. He was inside a house made of cardboard boxes and invited an older friend to join him. This second boy brought a book of matches. As they were playing with the matches the whole "house of boxes" became flames and Billy's clothes caught on fire. As this was occurring, Billy's mother was in the bedroom and knew nothing of what was happening. She suddenly became very hot and before her appeared an image of Billy with flames surrounding his body. She screamed and instantly ran out back to the field and smothered his clothes in the weeds, saving his life. Later she could not explain how or what she had experienced, except that she "saw" Billy on fire.

Post-mortem Apparitions are the basis for the scary tales of haunted houses. These Apparitions of the dead appear in more ghostly shapes than that of the crisis Apparitions who seem to be so real. Ghosts and ghost stories abound in our literature, dating back to the fifth century B.C. Apparitions or Ghosts which reappear, or are sighted in a certain location, are termed hauntings — thus the term "haunted house."

The general view of the early medieval Ghosts show a concern with establishing and following Christian teachings, whereas, the view of Ghosts in later years support the concept of life after death. This afterlife question is brought up by the appearance of Apparitions of the dead — often thought of as the person's soul or spirit. We humans are forever trying to convince ourselves that a part of us will live on after the death of the physical body. With this belief held close, perhaps our experience of Apparitions is that needed link between worlds to confirm the existence of life's eternity.

Poltergeist phenomena tend to occur when a child or adolescent is present. Poltergeist activity becomes the repeated movement of objects or spontaneous occurrences of psychokinesis (see PSYCHOKINESIS). Continual Poltergeist activity such as doors slamming, windows breaking, and objects being thrown could also be the result of an individual's incredible subconscious psychic ability.

Whether we believe in Ghosts or not, the question of the human personality continuing in a nonmaterial form after death of the physical body will continue to be an ever-reaching one until we grasp the understanding of a limitless world without timespace.

Recommended Reading

Auerbach, Loyd. *ESP, Hauntings & Poltergeists: A Parapsychologist's Handbook.* New York: Warner Books, 1986. "Everything you ever needed to know about the super-natural — but were too scared to ask!"

Finucane, R.C. *Appearances of the Dead: A Cultural History of Ghosts.* New York: Prometheus Books, 1984.

Jaffe, Aniela. *Apparitions.* Dallas, TX: Spring Publications, Inc., 1978. Pictures taken of actual sittings.

Manning, Matthew. *The Link.* New York: Holt, Rinehart & Winston, 1975. Experiences with Poltergeist phenomena

Mitchell, Edgar, editor. *Psychic Exploration.* New York: Putnam & Sons, 1974.

Owen, A.R.G. *Can We Explain the Poltergeist?* New York: Garrett Publishing, 1964. Survey of Poltergeist activity.

Rogo, D. Scott. *Mind Over Matter: The Case for Psychokinesis.* Great Britain: The Aquarian Press, 1986. History and studies of actual PK experiences.

Roll, William. *The Poltergeist.* New York: Doubleday & Co, Inc., 1972. Case studies and theory.

Tyrell, G.N. *Apparitions.* New York: Collier Books by The Society for Psychical Research, 1953. History and overview.

Aura

> *An AURA is the energizing halo or life-force which surrounds animate and inanimate objects. The human Aura is similar to a force-field protecting and emanating from every cell and organ of the body. This glowing energy has been called a "non-physical matrix," or "electric blue-print." The Aura's spiraling vibrational field can be seen, felt, and interpreted.*

Although some very sensitive people are acutely aware of auric colors, anyone can see or sense an Aura. Edgar Cayce described his ability:

> *Ever since I can remember I have seen colors in connection with people. I do not remember a time when the human beings I encountered did not register on my retina with blues and greens and reds gently pouring from their heads and shoulders. It was a long time before I realized that other people did not see these colors; it was a long time before I heard the word aura, and learned to apply it to this phenomenon which to me was commonplace.*

To read your own Aura, sit in a dimly lit room in front of a solid white or pale-colored wall, facing a mirror. The room should not be totally dark — candle light might be employed at night. Allow yourself at least ten minutes of total concentration. Focus on your forehead in the mirror without glancing to the side. It will take a few moments before you begin to sense a glow and can distinguish colors.

Some psychics profess there is more than one visible Aura, as many as seven have been identified within the "aural envelope," each with its own distinctive properties. An Aura may extend inches or several feet out from the body, and is colored according to the individual's current state of mental, emotional, physical, and spiritual health. Auras are most visible at the seven chakra centers (see CHAKRA).

Clear active colors indicate a positive state of being; conversely, if the colors are dull or stagnant, a negative influence is present. Sparks or flashes of color may be signals of events which will take place in your immediate future. Tears or holes in the auric field indicate illness.

Auric Colors and Interpretation

Gray, Black, Brown - negative disposition, depression, illness, bitterness, disease.

Red - high energy or restricted energy, passionate, quick to act, temperamental, possible blockage of emotion. This color can also represent change and the entering of a new phase.

Pink - uplifting, loving, child-like, loyal, cheerful.

Orange - thoughtful, mentally active, humanistic.

Yellow - high intellect, creative, logical, high spiritual potential, happy. Golden yellow represents unrealized spiritual attainment.

Green - love of nature, harmony, potential of love, nurturing. Emerald green indicates a healing ability or the need for healing.

Blue - teaching capacity, peaceful, idealistic, conservative and just. Bright clear blue means recognized spiritual development.

Indigo - highly intuitive, supersensitive, visionary, aesthetic, telepathic, futuristic.

Violet - imaginative, psychically sensitive, artistic, transformational power, an instinct for divine order.

White - harmony of self, integration of aspects of all colors.

Recommended Reading

Bowles, Barbara. *What Color is Your Aura?* New York: Pocket Books, 1989.

Brennan, Barbara Ann. *Hands of Light: A Guide to Healing Through the Human Energy Field.* New York: Bantam New Age Books, 1988. Suggests methods to see and interpret Auras.

Cayce, Edgar. *Auras.* Virginia Beach, VA: A.R.E. Press, 1945.

Hills, Christopher. *You Are a Rainbow.* Boulder Creek, CA: University of the Trees Press, 1979. Glimpse of Auric colors and their traits.

Regush, Nicholas, editor. *The Human Aura.* New York: Berkley Books, 1981. An update by several psychics, scientists, and philosophers.

Schwartz, Jack. *Human Energy Systems.* New York: E.P. Dutton, 1980. Everything you ever wanted to know about the human Aura.

Autogenics

> *AUTOGENICS is a form of training which utilizes the psychological pathways to modify behavior. It can be used in conjunction with other relaxation or self-hypnotic techniques to self-regulate the mind/body.*

While working with clients during hypnosis sessions, Johannes H. Schultz discovered that his clients experienced a wonderful freedom, warmth, and a heaviness in the limbs. Schultz then began training his clients to self-regulate this physically pleasant state themselves, inducing relaxation and automatic control of their psycho-physiological state. This technique has spread in knowledge and is now a form of therapy.

Autogenic Therapy includes the techniques of visualization, modification, neutralization, meditation, and various physical positions along with breathwork. As in biofeedback training (see BIOFEED-BACK), Autogenics strives to help the client observe his or her patterns of stress and tension, then ultimately teach the client to self-regulate the different areas of the mind/body connection to achieve optimum health and wholeness.

Progressive relaxation techniques are used in Autogenic Therapy to establish a state of total and complete relaxation. To induce this state of relaxation the client is asked to focus on a single muscle group at a time. The client is then directed to tense this area and to fully be aware of it. Lastly, the client is asked to totally release the muscle, release the hold on the tension, and release the focus. In this way the whole body is progressively relaxed. Autogenics assumes that when the client learns to master such techniques, stress, tension, pain, and so on can be automatically self-regulated. The underlying positive effect of Autogenics (as well as biofeedback, meditation, self-hypnosis, and mind power) is that the individual undergoing the therapy or training learns to discover the healer within.

Recommended Reading

Berkeley Holistic Health Center. *The New Holistic Health Handbook.* New York: Penguin Books, 1985. Complete overview.

Lindermann, Hannes. *How to Overcome Stress the Autogenic Way.* Germany: Berpelsmann, 1973.

Luthe, Wolfgang. *Introduction to the Methods of Autogenic Therapy.* New York: Grune & Stratton, 1977. For the professional.

Luthe, Wolfgang, and Johannes Schultz. *Autogenic Therapy.* New York: Grune & Stratton, NY, 1976.

Mason, L. John. *Guide to Stress Reduction.* Berkeley: Celestial Arts, 1980. Practical guide to establishing a program for Autogenics and stress reduction.

Pelletier, Kenneth. *Holistic Medicine: From Stress to Optimum Health.* New York: Dell Publishing Co., 1979. Historical and medical look at Autogenics.

Rosa, Karl. *You and A.T. —Autogenic Training.* New York: Dutton, 1976.

Chakra

Chakra

> *The word CHAKRA in Sanskrit means "wheel," which is how some have observed these life-force centers. There are seven chakras or centers in the human body that run parallel to the spine, extending from the base of the spine to the top of the head. These points are valves for the inflow and outflow of life energy and each joins one's auric energy to the physical body.*

One popular way of conceptualizing the Chakra system is as follows: The *first Chakra*, called the root Chakra, is located at the base of the spine and is associated with the gonads (sex glands). The *second Chakra*, situated mid-point in the abdomen, is related to the spleen (also the liver and pancreas). The *third Chakra* correlates with the adrenal glands in the solar plexus region where anxiety or fear may collect to create health and stomach problems.

The heart center is the *fourth Chakra* from which all energies are filtered to and from the life-force. This is the center representing unconditional love (see UNCONDITIONAL LOVE) and the first of the higher creative levels.

The *fifth Chakra* is the throat Chakra and is associated with the thyroid gland. When the fifth center is blocked (because of repressed communication or tension) neckaches, headaches, and throat discomfort are common symptoms. This energy center is also a channel for clairaudience (the ability, possessed by some sensitives, to hear the voices of nonphysical entities or spirits).

The *sixth and seventh Chakras* are located about the head. The sixth, in the middle of the forehead just above the brow line, relates to the pituitary gland. It is often referred to as the third eye (see THIRD EYE), or "the one eye of truth"; it represents spiritual potential. The seventh center is the crown Chakra, housed at the site of the pineal gland in the center of the crown. This Chakra is the point of potential union with the Higher-Self (see HIGHER-SELF) — its emanating energy is seen as the halo or ring of light about the heads of saints and religious teachers.

When all seven Chakras are functioning properly the body is attuned with the physical, mental, and spiritual aspects, and one experiences a sense of peace and well-being. However, if even one Chakra center is blocked, dull, or clouded with unprocessed energy (negativity), an individual is out of balance and his or her productive and creative capacity is adversely affected.

To help open or unblock any of the centers, use a simple technique called visualization (see VISUALIZATION). In a comfortable relaxed position with eyes closed, imagine each Chakra spinning energy, whirling like a pinwheel in a clockwise motion. Start with the first Chakra at the base of the spine. Examine the spin — if it is steady and regular, that Chakra is clear. Move up through the body to the next center, checking each for clarity and color. If one is dulled or sluggish, concentrate on cleansing or brightening its color and mentally spinning it faster. You should become gradually aware of an uplifting feeling or resurgence of energy. Continue to the next Chakra. When you reach the seventh, visualize a release of all negative energy or vibration out through the top of your head to equalize and open all the centers.

Recommended Reading

Anodea, Judith. *Wheels of Life.* St. Paul, MN: Llewellyn Publications, 1987. This book also has an accompanying cassette tape.

Dychtwald, Ken. *Body-Mind.* Los Angeles: J.P. Tarcher, Inc., 1981. Instruction book dealing with anatomy energy centers.

Gunther, Bernard. *Energy Ecstacy.* North Hollywood, CA: Newcastle Publishing Co., 1983. A comprehensive look at Chakras with illustration and easy exercises.

Joy, W.B. *Joy's Way.* Los Angeles: J.P. Tarcher, Inc., 1979. Healing through the energy system.

Leadbeater, C.W. *The Chakras.* Wheaton, IL: The Theosophical Publishing House, 1972.

Channel/Channeling

> A CHANNEL is a person able to receive thoughts, energies, or deeds from nonphysical entities, or consciousness from other levels of existence.

> CHANNELING is the transmission of communication from a level or dimension of reality other than the physical as we know it.

Seth, Emmanuel, Michael, Lazaris, Ramtha, Raphael, RA, Tom McPherson, and Agartha are just a few of the recognizable names from a growing list of channeled material. We seem to live in an era that encourages this phenomenon of connection and communication with other levels of consciousness. There are several valid theories which attempt to explain the experience of Channeling. Some well-known theories are: actual split or multiple personalities of the Channel; accessing the subconscious, higher conscious, or collective unconscious (see COLLECTIVE UNCONSCIOUS) realms of knowing; or the possibility of discarnate or spirit entities.

Outstanding Channels, such as Eileen Garrett, Mrs. Osborne Leonard, and Jane Roberts have dedicated themselves to investigating their Channeling experience and have been the subjects of much scientific and psychological testing. Eileen Garrett prefers to think of her Channeling as originating from her subconscious mind and not spiritual dwellers on the astral plane as they profess. Mrs. Leonard, on the other hand, believes her spirit guide, Feda, is just who she claims to be — her Hindu ancestor, not merely a dramatization of her subconscious-self.

Most Channels describe their experiences of Channeling in loving terms. They are not frightened by the experience, nor do they consider it a form of possession. Lazaris, Channeled by Jach Pursel, describes Channeling in the following way:

> In order to communicate with you, we send forth a series of vibrations. These vibratory frequencies go through a series of "step-down generations" until they can safely enter your reality [via the channel]. When we communicate we are not in the

body.... Such behavior is no more necessary than having your
nightly newscaster actually in your television set!

In Channeling, sensitives (see PSYCHIC/SENSITIVE) speak of shifting to another way of perceiving reality when they are in trance or starting to gain parapsychological insights. Somehow, an inner switch is turned on and their field of stimulation is changed. Jane Roberts described this shift in awareness when the Seth material was transmitted through her:

[It] is almost always an exhilarating experience, like riding some perfect gigantic ninth wave of energy,... Seth is that ninth wave of energy....his consciousness rises like some superreal mental creature from the tidal waves of a primal ocean of energy, so that he is himself and yet a part of a greater reality.... I sense the approach of that psychological surge. Then throwing off the clothes of my usual consciousness I mentally jump in, striking that wave at a certain point and making an intersection with it that results in the phenomenon of Seth as he appears in our sessions.

Trance Channel, Kevin Ryerson, believes that the medium's own psychology will attract the kind of entity that medium will Channel. "Like attracts like," he explains, "and ninety-nine percent of the time, with very few exceptions, the entity speaking through the Channel has a kind of simpatico or empathy with the Channel."

Although our science may never completely prove or disprove the actuality of discarnate souls speaking through physical mediums, some startling parapsychological and philosophical material has been produced in this manner. Exciting possibilities may be open to us if we explore and put to good use the often valuable information gained through Channeling, regardless of its origin. However, an important caution about Channeled material or superconscious insight is that it must first pass through the Channel's own subconscious mind. Even the purest message may become tainted in this process by the Channeler's own repressed psychological issues and bias. It is suggested that you keep a healthy skepticism alive; take responsibility for what *you* choose to believe; and ultimately, trust your own inner guidance.

The following criteria can be helpful in evaluating Channeled information: Does the Channeled material encourage my own personal power? Or, does it ask me to be a "follower" of the Channel? Can I use these teachings in a constructive way? Can I apply them to my everyday life? Is my life working better because of what I have learned? What does my *intuition* tell me about the Channeled material?

Recommended Reading

Kautz, William H., ScD., and Melanie Branon. *Channeling, the Intuitive Connection.* New York: Harper & Row, 1987. Foreword and Forecast by Kevin Ryerson.

Klimo, Jon. *Channeling.* Los Angeles: J.P. Tarcher, Inc., 1987. Well researched investigation.

LeShan, Lawrence. *The Medium, the Mystic, and the Physicist.* New York: The Viking Press, 1974.

Ridall, Kathryn. *Channeling.* New York: Bantam Books, 1988. A "how to" book for connecting with your spiritual essence and guides.

Roberts, Jane. *The God of Jane.* New York: Prentice-Hall, Inc., 1981. Comprehensive examination of mediumship and a thought provoking study of the multidimensional reality of Self.

Ryerson, Kevin, and Stephanie Harolde. *Spirit Communication: The Soul's Path.* New York: Bantam, 1989.

Smith, Susy. *The Mediumship of Mrs. Leonard.* New York: University Books, 1964.

Clairvoyance/Clairaudience

> *CLAIRVOYANCE is the ability to intuit events and see objects without the use of physical eyes.*

> *CLAIRAUDIENCE is the ability to hear without the use of physical ears.*

A Clairvoyant has the ability to harness the universal availability of the sixth sense, or ESP. Today the rise of Clairvoyant activity is due to the transformation of consciousness from an age of technology centering on the analytical left side of the brain to a more balanced nature drawing from not only the left but also the intuitive right side. Our present level of evolution inspires the joining of these two hemispheres of consciousness to encourage this balance.

Most of us at one time or another have used our Clairvoyant abilities. Think back to a time when you just "knew" the phone was going to ring — and it did! This is an indication of Clairaudience — hearing the phone ring with the sixth sense — or, Clairvoyance — seeing yourself go answer the phone in your mind's eye. Many instances of Clairvoyance have been recorded, some quite marvelous.

One type of Clairvoyance occurs when you have a dream, feeling, or vision about a distant event that is going on at the same time as the dream, feeling, or vision. Many people who have repeated Clairvoyant experiences decide not to share them with others for fear of being ridiculed. Be assured, if you are having psychic experiences of any kind, you are simply human and quite normal! Unexplainable Clairvoyant activity has been experienced throughout time and, hopefully, it will continue to increase, bringing a greater understanding of our intuitive nature.

Recommended Reading

Devereux, George. *Psychoanalysis and the Occult.* Berkeley: University of California Press, 1970.

Garrett, Eileen. *Many Voices: An Autobiography of a Medium.* New York: Putnam & Sons, 1968.

Garrett, Eileen. *My Life as a Search for the Meaning of Mediumship.* Salem, NH: Ayer Co., 1975.

Jung, Carl G. Aniela Jaffe, editor. *Memories, Dreams, and Reflections.* New York: Pantheon, 1963.

LeShan, Lawrence. *The Clairvoyant Reality.* New York: Ballantine, 1975. A look at the ties between the different types of Clairvoyance and the scientific outlook.

Rhine, L. *The Hidden Channel of the Mind.* New York: W. Sloane Assoc., 1961. Individual case studies.

Surge, Thomas. *There is a River.* New York: Dell, 1970. Psychic Edgar Cayce's biography.

Deja Vu

DEJA VU is a French term meaning "already seen." It is the feeling that the present event or situation is duplicating an experience from the past.

Have you ever been stopped mid-sentence or mid-thought with an almost overwhelming mind and/or body sensation of having *already* experienced the event happening at that moment? If so, you share the good company of millions including, Henry Ford, General Patton, Ralph Waldo Emerson, and many notable others. Deja Vu experiences can be inexplicable, very realistic, unexpected, and often verifiable.

Reincarnation (see REINCARNATION) is said to account for many Deja Vu experiences. It could explain why meeting someone new, or visiting an historical location for the first time, ignites a vivid memory. Some Deja Vu experiences can be explained by precognitive dreams which gives one a hint of the future. By keeping a dream journal, one can many times determine if the Deja Vu experience is merely the recall of a dream or actually a glimpse of another incarnation.

Recommended Reading

Christie-Murray, David. *Reincarnation: Ancient Beliefs and Modern Evidence*. Great Britain: Prism Press, 1988. Interesting case histories on Deja Vu.

Neppe, Vernon, M.D. *Deja Vu*. Johannesburg, South Africa: University of Witwatersrand Press, 1981.

Dream Analysis

Dream Analysis

DREAM ANALYSIS is the process of interpreting dreams to gain greater personal understanding. Dream interpretation has been practiced throughout the world, its first recorded evidence dating back to the ancient civilizations of China and Egypt. An interest in dreams and dream analysis continued into the Renaissance. More recently, many modern schools of psychoanalysis and counseling therapies use this tool. Also, dreams are a major area of research among today's parapsychologists.

Dreams can be exciting, frightening, creative, romantic, inspirational, symbolic, illogical, prophetic, and can sometimes seem more real than reality. Chuang-Tzu expressed this paradox more than a thousand years ago: "One night, I dreamed I was a butterfly, fluttering here and there, content with my lot. Suddenly I awoke and I was Chuang-Tzu again. Who am I in reality? A butterfly dreaming that I am Chuang-Tzu, or Chuang-Tzu dreaming he was a butterfly?"

Dreams occur about every ninety minutes during sleep, a cycle referred to as REM (rapid eye movement), and take up approximately two hours for every eight hours of sleep, with the dream cycles lengthening towards the end of the sleeping period. In a REM state one's blood pressure increases, face and hand muscles twitch, breathing becomes irregular or strained, and the eyes move rapidly back and forth under the eyelids as if one were viewing a scene from a film.

Drugs, sleeping pills, alcohol, and excessive amounts of caffeine can reduce the dreaming process, limiting one's ability to receive messages from the unconscious mind. Dreaming increases during periods of hardship or life crisis, becoming a therapeutic method to aid recovery and help the decision-making process. Even unremembered, dreams are a viable source of communication with the unconscious mind.

Dreams may seem difficult to interpret at first because they use a symbolic or pictorial language. Further, visual images that flash across the mind's eye mean different things to different dreamers. Catch phrases one uses to symbolize feelings are also incorporated in dream language, therefore; dreaming of a bridge during a crisis period may refer to a "bridge over troubled waters," and indicate that the dreamer is about to "bridge" his or her time of difficulty. Many common sayings become metaphors in dream language: The phrase "missing the boat," for example, may be the source of a Dream in which one does in fact miss a boat, or a message that the dreamer is missing out on an important opportunity.

About 80 percent of all Dreams are in color, the rest in shades of black and white or grey and brown. For persons blind since birth without visual references, Dreams are likely to include symbolic sounds or smells.

According to Carl Jung:

We dream in symbols because it is the language of the unconscious. We think and feel in symbols because we are bombarded by visual images in our waking hours. These are registered by our unconscious mind and stored in our mental depths, many of these images resurface during our dreams in connection with many specific problems or thoughts we had at the time we saw that particular thing.

The unconscious mind, sometimes called the "sleeping giant within us," has the ability to explore on a deeper level the day-to-day problems faced by the dreamer. This is why "sleeping on a problem" allows the dreamer a refreshed point of view and the possibility of receiving guidance to solve a difficult situation.

Dreams often fail to indicate past, present, or future. They do not follow a linear time sequence as does waking reality: The human unconscious moves in a space/time continuum where all things exist simultaneously.

Personal Dream Interpretation

Most Dreams have significance only to the individual dreamer, but there are some archetypal (see ARCHETYPAL SYMBOLS) motifs such as flying, weddings, swimming, falling, and some symbols like colors or numbers that have universal meaning and represent, in most cases, the same thing. Dream dictionaries list Dream symbols and their meanings, but far more significant is one's *personal* interpretation of Dream symbols. Every Dream is custom-fit with symbols that are the dreamer's own.

Keeping a Dream journal is a valuable method for discovering one's own Dream themes and symbols. Dreams should be transcribed immediately upon waking, for Dream memory is usually fleeting. If you are rushed in the morning, jot down a key word or two to jar your memory when you do have time to analyze it.

The very process of becoming interested in understanding and recording one's Dreams so delights the unconscious that it begins to provide more frequent and more memorable Dreams for consideration. In reviewing a Dream, ask your unconscious mind the Dream's meaning and allow your mind to wander freely over the various parts of the Dream: the characters, the setting, the objects, the situation. This recollection will trigger conscious associations. Trust these first thoughts that pop into your consciousness.

Many dreamers ask the unconscious to provide an answer through a Dream to a troublesome situation or problem by speaking out loud exactly what it is they want to discover. It may take several nights before the answer is communicated, and when it comes it will have to be decoded, but the unconscious mind rarely turns down such requests.

Sometimes you can encourage the unconscious to speak in symbols you will be sure to recognize and understand. Participants in a Dream workshop used the technique of writing down in their Dream journals a question to which the unconscious mind could answer with a yes or no, and asked that "yes" be indicated by the color white, and "no" be represented by the color black. Then they shared their black and white Dream images in group discussion. One dreamer posed a yes and no question regarding a difficult relationship and dreamed she was folding and putting away stacks of "white" linen. Another participant used this method and dreamed several consecutive Dreams about white porcelain sinks. In both cases, the dreamers later reported a successful outcome when they followed their Dream's affirmative recommendation.

Dreams can provide more than answers; many inventions, works of art, and successful concepts originate from Dreams. In the Dream state normal ego defenses and subconscious blockages are weakened. The creative dreamer is able to reach out in a state of heightened awareness, touch a higher creative self and grasp a cure, prophecy, or some valuable insight found within a Dream's message. German chemist F.A. Kekule discovered the proper structural formula for the benzene ring in a dream:

I turned the chair to the fireplace and sank into a half-sleep. The atoms flitted before my eyes....wriggling and turning like snakes.... One of the snakes seized its own tail and the image whirled scornfully before my eyes. As though from a flash of lightening I awoke. I occupied the rest of the night working out the consequences of the hypothesis.

At a scientific convention in 1890 Kekule advised, "Learn to Dream, gentlemen."

Recommended Reading

Bethards, Betty. *The Dream Book: Symbols for Self-Understanding.* Tiburon, CA: Inner Light Foundation, 1983. Unique in Dream dictionaries, sensitive and highly insightful.

Coxhead, David, and Susan Hiller. *Dreams.* New York: Crossroad, 1976. Enjoyable reading, includes illustrations.

Crisp, Tony. *Do You Dream?* New York: E.P. Dutton, 1972. A complete Dream guide.

Delaney, Gayle. *Living Your Dream.* New York: Harper & Row, 1979. Creative ideas for Dreams.

Garfield, Patricia. *Creative Dreaming.* New York: Ballantine Books, 1974. A classic.

Krippner, Stanley, and Joseph Dillard. *Dreamworking: How to Use Your Dreams for Creative Problem-Solving.* New York: Bearly Limited, 1988.

LaBerge, Stephen. *Lucid Dreaming.* New York: Ballantine Books, 1985. Learn to control your Dreams and heal your life.

Ullman, Montague, and Nan Zimmerman. *Working with Dreams.* New York: Dell Publishing, 1979.

Extra-Sensory Perception (ESP)

ESP stands for "extra-sensory perception;" or that which lies beyond the senses of sight, touch, taste, hearing, and smelling.

All realms of ESP lie beyond what we have labeled the "normal senses." Individually, ESP includes the forms of psychic phenomena found in the "Psychic Window" Section. Telepathy, Precognition, and Clairvoyance (see Individual Headings) are forms of Extra-Sensory Perception.

Recommended Reading

Huson, Paul. *How to Test and Develop Your ESP.* New York: Stein & Day Publishers, 1975. Exercises for developing ESP.

Mitchell, Edgar, editor. *Psychic Exploration.* New York: G.P. Putnam & Sons, 1974. Thorough examination of ESP.

Rhine, L. *The Hidden Channel of the Mind.* New York: W. Sloane Assoc., 1961. Collection of ESP case studies.

Rhine, L. *The Invisible Picture.* New York: McFarland & Co., Inc., 1981. Easy reading.

Stevens, Petey. *Opening Up to Your Psychic Self.* Berkeley: Nevertheless Press, 1987. Exercises and demonstrations to help develop psychic abilities.

Swann, Ingo. *Natural ESP.* New York: Bantam Books, 1987. A layman's guide.

Targ, Russell, and Harold Puthoff. *Mind-Reach.* New York: Dell Publishing, 1978. Recent research into our latent powers of ESP.

Thurston, Mark. *Understand and Develop Your E.S.P.* Virginia Beach, VA: The A.R.E. Press, 1977. (May be out of print.)

Spiritual Emergence Network, California Institute of Transpersonal Psychology, 250 Oak Grove Ave., Menlo Park, CA 94025. (415) 327-2776. An international "hot line" for individuals in psychic or spiritual crisis.

John F. Kennedy University Graduate School for the Study of Human Consciousness, 12 Altarinda Road, Orinda, CA 94563. (415) 254-0200. A university program for the Study of Human Consciousness with facilities for research and experimentation in the realm of psi phenomena.

Inspirational/Automatic Writing

INSPIRATIONAL and AUTOMATIC WRITING describe a means of communication whose source is other than the writer's conscious mind. In the case of Inspirational Writing, the source is presumed to be the subconscious or higher conscious mind; Automatic Writing identifies communication believed to be from a subject totally removed from the writer.

For many people, *good* writing is always Inspirational, a process by which the pen becomes a channel from the author's subconscious to the page. When the creative force comes from outside the writer the experience is a little different. William Blake, writing his epic poem, "Milton," described it this way: "I have written this poem from immediate dictation, twelve or sometimes to thirty lines at a time, without premeditation, and even against my will."

There are more extreme incidents of Automatic Writing in which volumes have been produced. The Society for Psychical Research attempts to verify cases in which languages unknown to the writer have been written automatically. Mrs. Pearl Curran is a well known case of Automatic Writing. Her experience began with a message transmitted by Ouija board: "Many moons ago I lived. Again I come. Patience Worth is my name." Sometime following that first communication, Mrs. Curran, a St. Louis housewife with an eighth-grade education, began writing messages from Patience Worth. Four books, as well as short stories, poetry, plays, articles, and essays resulted. These works were all acclaimed by literary critics as genius in written expression, wit, and philosophical thought.

Pearl Curran wrote over a million and a half words "dictated" by Patience Worth. Most remarkable is that Patience Worth's "dictation" was in sixteenth-century English with a high percentage of Anglo-Saxon dialect unknown to Mrs. Curran. In his study, *The Case of Patience Worth*, parapsychologist Walter F. Prince concludes: "Either our concept of what we call the subconscious mind must be radically altered so as to include potencies of which we hitherto had no knowledge, or else some cause operating through, but not originating in, the subconscious of Mrs. Curran must be acknowledged."

Automatic or Inspirational Writing occurs spontaneously, but may be induced. To induce Inspirational Writing have the tools at hand, a pen, pencil, or typewriter (whichever is most comfortable), then consider a topic or some area of your life you would like to explore. If you find it difficult to get started, another technique suggests that you begin writing the letters of the alphabet, at the same time allowing your mind to wander. If you are successful, your pen will move in conjunction with your inner thoughts or actually proceed on its own.

To distinguish between Inspirational Writing (from the subconscious) and Automatic Writing (from an outside source) it is recommended the writer attempt to engage his or her conscious mind in an activity other than the writing. If one is able to carry on a conversation, or read, or plan a dinner party while the pen continues to move across the page, one may assume he or she is experiencing Automatic Writing.

Recommended Reading

Manning, Mathew. *The Link.* New York: Rinehart & Winston, 1975. Fascinating experiences with poltergeist phenomena, Automatic Writing, and Automatic Drawing.

Montgomery, Ruth. *Strangers Among Us.* New York: Fawcett Crest Books, 1981.

Montgomery, Ruth. *Threshold to Tomorrow.* New York: G.P. Putnam & Sons, 1983.

Montgomery, Ruth. *A World Before.* New York: Fawcett Crest Books, 1984.

Intuition

INTUITION comes from the Latin word "intuire," which means "knowing from within." It is the name we give to those moments of "divine clearness" or "forward-looking," whether personal, worldly, aesthetic or philosophical in nature.

Intuition in ancient times was thought of as messages from the gods, given to a chosen few. The most advanced of humankind, from Plato to Jung, from the Oracle of Delphi to Nostradamus, from the Egyptian diviners to Einstein, and from the Taoist monks to the Christian mystics, have sought to explain and discover this secret way of knowing the unknowable. Plotinus theorized that Intuition went beyond the intellectual processes and was larger than rational comprehension. Aristotle believed in "intuitive reason" and felt it to be "more accurate than scientific knowledge."

Michael Polanyi studied the prominent role of intuition in "breakthrough" discoveries by contemporary scientists. Wigner, a Nobel physicist, feels that logic comes after intuition. Johann Friedrich Karl Gauss, the famous mathematician, discussed this dilemma of logic following intuition, "I have had my solutions for a long time, but I do not yet know how I am to arrive at them."

In her book, *Awakening Intuition*, Francis Vaughan explains the unlimited power of intuition in helping us with problem solving and discovery:

Intuition allows one to draw on that vast storehouse of unconscious knowledge that includes not only everything that one has experienced or learned, either consciously or subliminally but also the infinite reservoir of the collective or universal unconsciousness, in which individual separateness and ego boundaries are transcended.

There are four levels of intuitive experience; physical, emotional, mental, and spiritual. The physical level encompasses body awareness or a strong body sense such as "gut feeling," chills, or tingling sensations. This level of Intuition may warn a person to avoid impending danger. The emotional level of Intuition is cued to conscious awareness through feelings, and emotional sensitivity to energies or "vibes" (see VIBRATIONAL ENERGY/TONAL RESONANCE). The mental level of Intuition comes to awareness through images, symbols, and intuitive flashes or inspiration. Intuition occurs from this mental level when thoughts are so crystal clear you *know* the right answer or action to take, this "hunch" becomes an intuition-based thought. The spiritual level of intuition is the ground-core from which all other forms of Intuition originate. It is independent of sensation, feelings, and thoughts and is associated with mystical experience.

Spiritual teacher Sri Aurobindo felt that intuition is a *memory* of the truth. You can enhance and develop this access to truth by using techniques which encourage relaxation, quieting of the mind, concentration and focusing of attention, and being receptive to images that open the intuitive focus.

Recommended Reading

Gawain, Shakti. *Living in the Light.* San Rafael, CA: New World Library, 1986. A guidebook for learning how to trust your Intuition.

Goldberg, Philip. *The Intuitive Edge.* Los Angeles: J.P. Tarcher, Inc., 1976. Down to earth and informational.

Inglis, Brian. *The Unknown Guest:* The Mystery of Intuition. Pennsylvania: Coronet Books, 1989.

Rosanoff, Nancy. *Intuition Workout.* New York: Aslan Publishing, 1988.

Smith, Ross. *Eureka! The Six Stages of Creativity.* Middletown, CA: Harbin Springs Publishing, 1988. Workbook to stimulate creativity and intuition.

Tower, Virginia. *The Process of Intuition.* Wheaton, IL: The Theosophical Publishing House, 1987.

Vaughan, Francis. *Awakening Intuition.* New York: Anchor Press/ Doubleday, 1979. Filled with exercises to open the inward sight.

Kirlian Photography

KIRLIAN or HIGH VOLTAGE PHOTOGRAPHY uses a burst of high voltage electricity at high frequency to photograph an object's aura. Kirlian Photography displays colorful, glowing energy waves surrounding the item photographed.

The Kirlian process was developed in 1939 by Valentine and Semyon Kirlian, a husband and wife research team in the Soviet Union. The United States did not pursue investigating their method of capturing auric radiance on film until the 1970's. Kendal Johnson, the first American to build Kirlian equipment, refers to the process as photographing the "non-material reality."

Many of the first Kirlian experiments were performed using leaves as subjects. A Kirlian Photograph of a recently severed leaf sometimes resembles a Christmas tree lit with dots and bubbles of sparkling color and light. Over a period of days, successive Kirlian photographs show significant deterioration of both color and brightness. After several days, even though the leaf still looks physically healthy, only a dim picture can be obtained. Most scientists believe this is due to the lack of moisture, heat, and weight in a dead leaf — the three major determinants of the "Kirlian field."

One startling discovery of Kirlian Photography was the "phantom leaf" effect. In this case the experimenter snipped off a portion or tip of a leaf, and then photographed it. In some of the resulting prints the photograph portrayed a leaf that was still whole. This phenomenon has not been thoroughly explained, however, many believe that the resulting picture is capturing what Harold S. Burr termed the "BOM," standing for biological organizing model found around each organism. In his book, *The Fields of Life*, Burr called this concept a "force field."

Kirlian Photographs have been taken before and after the "laying on of hands" by spiritual healers. In some cases, the healer's luminous fingertip corona is much larger and brighter than the patient's in the "before" shot, and the reverse is true after the healing attempt has been completed. The Kirlian process has also been successful in disease detection often *before* there is any physiological evidence of cancer and certain other illnesses.

Recommended Reading

Dakin, H.S. *High-Voltage Photography.* San Francisco: H.S. Dakin Publisher, 1975. For the mechanical-minded reader.

Davis, Mikol, and Earle Lanc. *Rainbows of Life Energy.* New York: Harper & Row, 1978. Colorfully illustrated.

Krippner, Stanley. *Human Possibilities: Mind Research in the USSR and Eastern Europe.* New York: Anchor Books, 1980.

Krippner, Stanley. *The Kirlian Aura: Photographing the Galaxies of Life.* First Edition, New York: Anchor Books, 1974.

Moss, Thelma. *The Body Electric.* Los Angeles: J.P. Tarcher, Inc., 1979. An exciting look at Kirlian Photography.

Near-Death Experience (NDE)

A NEAR-DEATH EXPERIENCE (NDE) is a term used to describe an out-of-body-awareness during the event of an imminent bodily death.

Well-documented perceptions incountered in Near-Death Experiences include: a sensation of separation from one's body; a passage through a dark tunnel or void; an encounter with a being of Light; for adults, a review of one's life; the discovery of a boundary of some sort which cannot be crossed; sensing a world of supernatural beauty; and the decision (or command) to go back to earth.

NDEs are being researched to help us discern whether they are an actual glimpse of the astral plane. Psychologist Kenneth Ring rigorously studied NDEs and concluded that "...the NDE may well be a relatively insignificant arrow pointing to a view of reality that will revolutionize our thinking." He continues:

Near-death research has forced us to confront some aspects of human experience which naturally lead us to go beyond currently acceptable scientific formulations of reality. That encompassing vision of reality is of greater significance than what points to it.... If NDEs have served to awaken us to this transcendent vision of life, they will have amply rewarded our attention to them.

Whether an NDE is an actual glimpse of the reality of "life after death" will be questioned by scientists until the concept of death (see DEATH) has been clarified.

Many children have reported NDEs and have kept within the basic stages of perception related by adults except for the "life review." This would seem appropriate since children have few life experiences to review. There is a case of a two year old boy who, after biting into an electrical cord, exhibited no heartbeat or respiration for twenty-five minutes. Months later, after having learned to see, walk, and talk again, he told his mother what had happened during his near-death episode. He said that he entered a room with a bright light. There was a man who asked him if he wished to stay there. He chose to go home.

This near-death story (and the one written in the Individual Heading of DEATH), makes it hard *not* to believe in a "life after death" concept. Ring claims boldly that the only satisfactory explanation of the NDE phenomenon "...is one which accepts a nonphysical, transcendent reality."

Recommended Reading

Gabbard, Glen O., and Stuart W. Tremlow. *With the Eyes of the Mind.* New York: Praeger Press, 1985. OBEs and NDEs studied in relationship to the mind/body perceptions in psychiatry.

Moody, Raymond. *Life After Life.* Harrisburg, PA: Stackpole Books, 1987.

Moody, Raymond. *The Light Beyond.* New York: Bantam Books, 1988.

Meyers, Frederick W. *Human Personality & Its Survival of Bodily Death.* Salem, NH: Ayer Co. Publishers, Inc., 1975. Classic works on NDEs.

Osis, Karlis, and Erlendur Haraldson. *At the Hour of Death.* New York: Hastings Press, 1986. A cross-cultural survey of NDEs.

Ring, Kenneth. *Heading Toward Omega: In Search of the Meaning of the Near-Death Experience.* New York: William Morrow & Co., 1984. Investigating the meaning of NDEs.

Wake, Wilma. *Beyond the Body.* New York: Leisure Books, 1983.

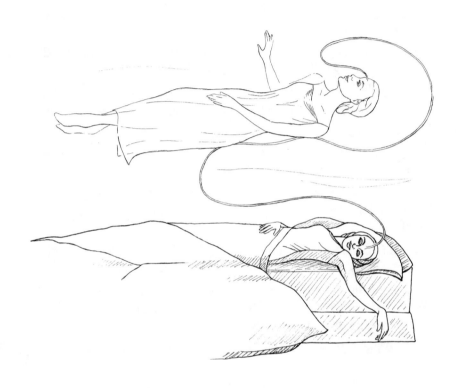

Out-of-Body Experience (OBE)

Out-of-Body Experience (OBE)

An OUT-OF-BODY EXPERIENCE (OBE), also called astral traveling, is the experience of perceiving external events or objects from a location that seems to be above or beyond one's physical body. Many people believe that it is the separation of the soul or etheric body from its physical body. The OBE phenomenon has been recorded throughout history.

It is calculated that as many as one in five people will experience an OBE in their lifetime. The conditions of crisis, illness, or accident may contribute to the initiation of an OBE, as in the numerous cases of persons pronounced clinically dead and later revived who can recount the experience (which are also called near-death-experiences). The following is actor Peter Sellers'account of his heart attack, as recorded by Shirley MacLaine in her book *Out On A Limb*:

...I just floated out of my physical form and I saw them cart my body away to the hospital.... I wasn't frightened or anything like that because I was fine; and it was my body that was in trouble.... Rex [the doctor] felt my pulse and saw that I was dead.... [He] commanded somebody to carve me open right there on the spot. I was so curious watching him.... Then I looked around myself and I saw an incredibly beautiful bright loving white light above me....I knew there was love, real love, on the other side of the light....I tried to elevate myself toward it as Rex was working on my heart. Then I saw a hand reach through the light. I tried to touch it, to grab onto it, to clasp it so it could sweep me up and pull me through it. Then I heard Rex below me,... "I'm getting a heartbeat." At the same moment a voice attached to the hand I wanted to touch so much said,... "Go back and finish. It's not time".... I felt myself floating back into my body. I was bitterly disappointed. After that I don't remember anything until I regained consciousness back inside my body.

Like Sellers, many people who have had an OBE report with amazing detail what their astral body sees. Under controlled conditions subjects have given verified accurate descriptions of objects, persons, and places seen in their out of body travels. Some astral experiences begin with a "foggy" feeling until one has adjusted to this new state. After the adjustment, one feels alert, mobile, exceptionally sensitive and aware of every detail. A number of people have described a silvery or glowing cord connecting their astral body to their physical body's third eye (the area in the middle of the forehead). At the moment the two bodies are reunited, some of these individuals describe the feeling as a jolt or snap.

OBEs may be experienced as a hovering above the physical body or as a high-speed journey of various lengths. Several cases have been recorded in which the subjects claim having projected themselves into non-material stratas — places where souls pass over into realms occupied by highly evolved or spiritually developed entities.

OBEs have been reported by people from all walks of life and do not seem to favor a particular race or gender; however, a higher incidence is reported among men and women between the ages of twenty to thirty-five. Admittedly, inducing an OBE is difficult. Fear may be the biggest cause of failure — fear of the unknown, or of not being able to return to the physical body. But there are a variety of methods recommended to try, most of which require visualization (see VISUALIZATION), such as imagining spinning and spiraling up from your body, or picturing yourself whirling through a tunnel and flying out the other side.

Another technique is to relax in a reclining position, then consciously command your soul body to project up out of your physical body and at the same time visualize the experience. Since the feeling of flying in a dream is similar to an OBE, asking for such a dream may set up the right psychological condition to start the soul's ascent.

Recommended Reading

Blackmore, Susan. *Beyond the Body: An Investigation of Out-of-the-Body Experiences.* New York: Academy Chicago Press, 1989.

Fox, Oliver. *Astral Projection.* New York: Citadel Press, 1974. Explores detailed accounts of OBEs and techniques to initiate this experience.

Gabbard, Glen O. and Stuart W. Twemlow. *With the Eyes of the Mind.* New York: Praeger, 1985. OBEs studied in relationship to the mind/body principal.

Greenhouse, H. B. *The Astral Journey.* New York: Avon Books, 1976.

Monroe, Robert A. *Journeys Out of the Body.* New York: Anchor Press/Doubleday, 1977. Fascinating case studies.

Plumly, Stanley. *Out of the Body Travel.* New York: Ecco Press, 1978. In-depth.

Parapsychology/Paranormal (PSI)

> *PARAPSYCHOLOGY is the branch of science that studies paranormal phenomena, such as, extra-sensory perception (ESP), psychokinesis (PK), out-of-body-experiences (OBE), channeling and spiritual phenomena.*

> *A PARANORMAL experience is a phenomenon that defies logical explanation and has no attributable physical cause. "Psi" is the twenty-third letter of the Greek alphabet and designates the unknown. The term psi is now internationally used to represent psychic phenomena in general.*

In 1969 the Parapsychological Association, which was formed in 1957, was admitted to affiliate membership in the American Association for the Advancement of Science. Historically, parapsychology has drawn the intense interest of many great scientists. Three Nobel laureates, Lord Rayleigh, Charles Richet, and J.J. Thompson were among the first officers of Britain's renowned Society for Psychical Research. Alexis Carrel, the Curies, Schroedinger, Max Planck, Charles Sherrington, John Eccles, and Brian Josephson were other Nobel laureates who were interested in psi. The "Father of American Psychology," as William James has been described, also co-founded the American Society for Psychical Research.

The word Parapsychology — which was introduced in Germany in the nineteenth century — literally means "beyond" psychology. However, its studies are not related to psychology alone, but include anthropology, biology, religion, theology, and physics, as well as other areas. Psi concepts such as, mind over matter, life after death, and spirit communication antedate the earliest recorded history of the ancient civilizations of Babylonia, Assyria, and China. In the world today, a growing number of people are reporting an increase in psychic abilities and paranormal phenomena.

Archaeologists, police departments, and stock brokers have made frequent use of psychics and clairvoyants. Mining and oil companies have employed psychics with most rewarding results. The U.S.S.R.

and the United States have both supported an active interest in the *military* applications of psychic phenomena. Since the early 1920's, the Soviet Union has officially sponsored psi research in all areas, however, American parapsychology laboratories still struggle for acceptance and funding.

Philosopher and author, C.W. Leadbeater, once said, "It is one of the most common of mistakes to consider that the limit of our power of perception is also the limit of all there is to perceive." Parapsychology, modern physics, and paraphysics (the study of the physics of paranormal process) are steadily moving closer together help us understand our relationship with the rest of the universe. Hopefully, these three sciences will continue to complement one another with greater clarity and encourage conceptual changes in all fields of science.

Recommended Reading

Auerbach, Loyd. *ESP, Hauntings and Poltergeists: A Parapsychologist's Handbook.* New York: Warner Books, 1986. Deep research into psi with intriguing case histories.

Douglas, Apryl J. *Developing Psychic Abilities.* California: TEC Publications, 1987.

Ebon, Martin, editor. *The Signet Handbook of Parapsychology.* New York: A Signet Book, 1978. Collection of essays.

Eisenbud, Jule, M.D. *Parapsychology and the Unconscious.* Berkeley: North Atlantic Books, CA, 1983.

Gittleson, Bernard. *Intangible Evidence.* New York: Simon & Schuster, Inc., 1987. An extensive exploration of psychic phenomena with exercises for developing one's psychic skills.

Mitchell, Edgar D., editor. *Psychic Exploration.* New York: G.P. Putnam & Sons, 1974. 708 pages and packed to the brim.

Rogo, Scott D. *Psychic Breakthroughs Today.* Great Britian: The Aquarian Press, 1987. An examination of the latest in psi.

Roll, William, and Stanley Krippner, editors. *Advances in Parapsychological Research.* New York: McFarland & Co. Publishing, Inc., 1987. In-depth research of Parapsychology.

For further information on various Parapsychological data and research you may write to: The American Society for Psychical Research, 5 West 73rd Street, New York, NY 10023.

John F. Kennedy University Graduate Program for the Study of Human Consciousness, 12 Altarinda Road, Orinda, CA 94563. (415) 254-0200. A university program for the Study of Human Consciousness with facilities for research and experimentation in the realm of psi phenomenon.

Precognition

> *PRECOGNITION is a foreknowledge through any means, with no apparent present data available, of an event which ultimately transpires.*

The word Precognition comes from the words "cognition," that pertaining to conscious awareness, and the prefix "pre" that which precedes. Precognition, then, becomes a conscious awareness of an event which precedes its conclusion.

Precognition surfaces in many forms. Instances of Precognition can also occur in an altered state of consciousness, or trance (see ALTERED STATES OF CONSCIOUSNESS). Precognitive dreams are quite common, although many people do not discuss this ability openly. Parapsychological research relates one such experience of a woman who dreamed she saw a car catching on fire and exploding. On the following day she came upon a crowd surrounding the burning remains of a taxi; she was told it had just exploded when its gas tank caught on fire.

Lives have been saved because of the occurrence of Precognitive flashes of insight. Cases of people seeing a vision of a violent accident, or dreaming of a devastating storm have been accurately documented. It is when these precognitive scenes are *not* heeded that destruction has followed.

We can also look to the past in what is termed "retrocognition," or the ability to experience or sense what was occurring in a past time with no actual present memory of that time. A case in point would be someone who lives in 1988 and experiences and "relates" past events of 1888 as if he/she were actually in that time period. These instances are not as common and are rarely reported to investigators of parapsychology.

Precognition questions the concept of time. Could there be no firm barriers between past, present, and future after all? If one can foresee the future, is the future already happening? Questions like these will be asked until we gain the insight to unfold the mysteries of the universe; until that time, we can share and investigate our premonitions with each other and offer understanding to those who remain skeptical.

Recommended Reading

Eisenbud, Jule, M.D. *Paranormal Foreknowledge: Problems & Perplexities.* New York: Human Science Press, 1982.

Houston, Jean. *The Possible Human.* Los Angeles: J.P. Tarcher, Inc., 1982. Exercises working with time/space and precognition.

Mitchell, Edgar, editor. *Psychic Exploration.* New York: G.P. Putnum & Sons, 1974. Complete look at precognition as well as other psi phenomena.

Osborn, Arthur W. *The Future is Now: The Sign of Precognition.* Rock Island, IL: Quest Publishing, 1967.

For further information on various parapsychological data and research you may write to: The American Society for Psychical Research, 5 West 73rd Street, New York, NY 10023.

Psychic/Sensitive

A PSYCHIC or SENSITIVE is a person who is able to induce a psychic experience or demonstrate ESP.

Everyone is Psychic to some degree. It is believed that this ability can be enhanced with practice. Psychics have delicate antennae that can tune into external stimuli and the subtle energies around them. From childhood, Sensitives often see colors and hear sounds more keenly than normal. If acutely sensitive, they may even "merge" with others, finding it difficult to distinguish between their own emotions and the foreign feelings they are picking up from others. Sensitivity to surrounding vibrational patterns is a gift meant to help us understand the physical and nonphysical aspects of our world.

In many cases, Sensitives combine a number of psychic, or ESP talents. A Psychic's skills may include trance diagnosis and reading of past lives. Some sensitives can even produce nonphysical voices directly on recording tape — an electronic equivalent of automatic writing. Uri Geller, one of the most controversial Psychics of our day, claims to be clairvoyant, telepathic, and to be able to affect objects by consciously directing his mind's energy. For an article in *New Realities* magazine, Jim Bolen conducted an interview with Uri Geller — his former wife Jean, a psychiatrist, and two scientists from Stanford Research Institute were also present. In her book, *The Tao of Psychology*, Jean Bolen writes of their experience during this interview:

In order to demonstrate psychokinesis (PK) or mind over matter, Uri offered to try to bend the hotel room's Schlage brass key by lightly stroking the metal and willing it to bend. As we watched, it did bend! Then Jim placed it on a piece of paper and outlined the angle of the bend. It lay on the coffee table, untouched by Geller or anyone else, observed by us all. And when we next checked it, the angle of the bend was more acute — the metal key had continued to bend.

Recommended Reading

Hoffman, Enid. *Develop Your Psychic Skills.* Pennsylvania: Whitford Press, 1981.

Hoffman, Enid. *Expand Your Psychic Skills.* North Carolina: Parapsychology Press, 1987. Techniques, exercises, games, and meditations to enhance your psychic development.

Levine, Fredrich G. *Psychic Sourcebook.* New York: Warner Books, 1988. How to choose a psychic.

Miller, Michael, and Josephine Harper. *The Psychic Energy Workbook.* New York: Sterling Publishing Co., 1987. Simple exercises to experience a variety of psychic phenomena.

Rogo, Scott D. *Our Psychic Potentials.* New York: Prentice-Hall, Inc., 1984. Written by an authority in the field.

John F. Kennedy University Graduate Program for the Study of Human Consciousness, 12 Altarinda Road, Orinda, CA 94563. (415) 254-0200. A university program for the Study of Human Consciousness with facilities for research and experimentation in the realm of psi phenomenon.

Spiritual Emergence Network, California Institute of Transpersonal Psychology, 250 Oak Grove Ave., Menlo Park, CA 94025. (415) 327-2776. An international "hot line" for individuals in psychic or spiritual crisis.

Psychokinesis (PK)

PSYCHOKINESIS (PK) is the act of influencing the outside world through pure thought, or mind power. It also refers to the phenomenon of objects moving without any known explanation.

In the book *Lifetide,* author and biologist Lyall Watson tells of his startling experience in Venice with a little girl named Claudia. It seems she had the amazing ability to turn an ordinary tennis ball inside-out using only the power of her mind. At five years old she was still too young to know such things were impossible, so to her it was merely a natural bit of fun. The tennis ball Claudia inverted before Watson's eyes still contained its pressurized air which let out a hiss when he cut through it with a knife. He writes:

I know enough of physics to appreciate that you cannot turn an unbroken sphere inside-out like a glove. Not in this reality.... And so my Un-tennis ball has become for me a sort of symbol. Another way of looking at things.... for anyone touched by magic, as I was in Venice, things can never be quite the same again.

Research in the area of PK indicates we all might have the inherent ability to tap into the powers that influence inanimate objects. Some students studying Psychokinesis are now using concentrative techniques to try bending spoons and move pencils across a table purely by thought. Also, studies have reported that a large fraction of the population can mentally influence the fall of dice.

PK and precognition (see PRECOGNITION) seem to be a goal-oriented process. Those with PK ability target the final outcome of an action, thereby, aiming to "see" the completed event in their mind's eye. If viewed in this manner, PK can be seen as a form of precognition or the foreknowledge of what the final event will be. Further research is needed to understand the relationship of these two goal-oriented psychic phenomena.

Psychokinesis is the basis for our understanding the phenomenon of poltergeists (see APPARITION/GHOST/POLTERGEIST). It is felt that these recurrent Psycho-kinetic acts of moving objects stem from the direction of a particular individual's mind power. The source of this unconscious act of levitation during the occurrence of poltergeist activity is, in many instances, a child or adolescent with incredible psychic energy.

A simple test of PK ability is to try to affect the direction of the hand on a compass, or move a paper match on a smooth table top using only your mental energy. If you are successful, let us know!

Recommended Reading

Forwald, H. *Mind, Matter, and Gravitation.* New York: The Parapsychology Foundation, 1969.

Krippner, Stanley. *Human Possibilities: Mind Research in the USSR and Eastern Europe.* New York: Anchor Books, 1980. Interesting case of Psychokinesis included.

Mitchell, Edgar D., editor. *Psychic Exploration.* New York: G. P. Putnam & Sons, 1974.

Rhine, L. *Mind Over Matter.* New York: Macmillan, 1970. Reports of PK with emphasis on meaningful coincidences.

Rogo, Scott D. *Mind Over Matter: The Case for Psychokinesis.* Great Britain: The Aquarian Press, 1986. History and studies of actual PK experiences.

Psychometry

PSYCHOMETRY is the art of touching or holding an object for the purpose of sensing impressions about its owner.

All animate and inanimate objects emit vibrations which may be perceived by one or more of the senses. Psychometry is the phenomenon of perceiving those vibrations by means of touch. Practiced by many professional psychics (see PSYCHIC/SENSITIVE), Psychometry has been used successfully in solving police cases, or "crime busting." This tactile method of psychic sensing can be used to provide descriptive information as well as information about the past, present, and future life experiences of the owner of the article being Psychometrized.

When an individual touches or holds an object, nerve endings in the fingers send signals to the brain describing the characteristics of the object. In addition, every item touched is supposedly left with a part of his or her own energy field just as one leaves fingerprints; each being unique to the individual. It is this lingering energy field or auric impression (see AURA) that can be picked up intuitively using Psychometry. Just as a person's aura contains data relating to his or her past, present, and future, so does the auric impression left on the objects he or she has touched.

It is difficult to distinguish between different energy fields imprinted on an item, such as keys which have been handled by several persons. It is best to use an object that has had only one owner or an item that evokes an emotional charge from the owner, such as a ring or piece of jewelry that has special meaning and will carry the auric imprint more strongly.

Persons with pronounced psychic ability may develop this technique more readily and accurately than the novice; however, anyone can encourage some degree of Psychometric talent. Utilize this technique to gather information about others and to sense your own possible future experiences. Through Psychometry you become your own personal psychic and can direct your life more positively.

Learning to Psychometrize objects can be both enlightening and a great deal of fun:

1. Hold a personal object in one or both hands, whichever feels most comfortable.

2. Relax and take a few deep breaths to release the stomach or solar plexus area. (This serves to enlarge your aura to overlap the object's aura). It is also suggested that visualizing a cylinder of light spiraling up from the top of the head or pituitary chakra (see CHAKRA) has a calming effect and will open one's intuitive channel.

3. Now allow a free flow of impressions to be felt. Learn to trust whatever comes into your mind and speak aloud what you are thinking or visualizing or feeling. A tape recorder is an excellent way to keep track of your impressions.

4. After these impressions end, start directing specific questions: How is my health? Will this or that project be successful? How am I being affected emotionally by a present experience or situation? You should glimpse intuitive answers to these questions. Trust them.

Practice is the key to developing Psychometric ability. One gains confidence as accuracy increases.

Recommended Reading

Bartlett, Laile E. *Psi Trek.* New York: McGraw-Hill Book Company, 1981. Covers several fields of psychic study with an interesting section on Psychometry.

Moss, Thelma. *The Probability of the Impossible.* Los Angeles: J.P. Tarcher, Inc., 1974. Tips on the art of Psychometry.

Remote Viewing (RV)

> *REMOTE VIEWING (RV), also called "Remote Sensing," is a natural psychic ability to accurately sense or imagine an object, location, or event randomly chosen by a second person.*

As a child did you ever play the game where someone hid a toy or other object while you were in another part of the house or yard, then you had to go find it — or, perhaps you enjoyed the traditional "Easter egg hunt." These types of childhood games are very close to what has been termed in parapsychology as Remote Viewing, or RV.

An example of RV is when one person named the "viewer" goes out of sensory distance of a second person, the "beacon," who is holding an object or "target." The viewer must use his/her inner viewing abilities to accurately describe or draw a picture of the object being held. Another example is to have the beacon go to a particular location or event while the viewer tries to describe or draw the target site or the surrounding circumstances. One successful experiment (among many) of RV was conducted when the viewer correctly drew a picture of the location where the beacon was standing and it was thirty miles away.

Remote Viewing is a psychic ability which uses telepathy, precognition, and/or clairvoyance (see TELEPATHY, PRECOGNITION, CLAIRVOYANCE/CLAIRAUDIENCE) to discern mentally what is happening at a distance, or in a future instance. An easy exercise to test Remote Viewing skills is to have a friend randomly choose a picture of a certain country or area and hold it in their hands. You, being the viewer, station yourself in another room, relax, and try to pick up mentally what the scene in the picture portrays. Sense carefully how the scene feels — what are the colors and the smells of the area? Wait until you feel you could draw it on a piece of paper in front of you, then do so. You just might be amazed with the results!

Recommended Reading

Targ, Russell, and Keith Harary. *The Mind Race.* New York: Villard Books, 1984. Complete overview of Remote Viewing.

Telepathy

Telepathy

> *TELEPATHY is a form of ESP which involves extra-sensory communication through imagery, thoughts, or feelings between the minds of two persons, and not through ordinary communication patterns.*

The use of Telepathy, or as some call it, "mental telepathy," is becoming more accepted in today's society. Telepathy has been studied through research experiments exploring whether certain people *can* transmit or receive messages psychically. Actually, all of us have this telepathic ability, however, it takes much patience and practice to *accurately* communicate telepathically.

One might ask why it takes training to use this innate faculty. Just as with any new venture, the conscious action toward it stimulates the effort, but it is with relaxation and mind control (see MIND POWER) that our desires are brought into reality. Relaxation (not concentration) opens these channels and mind control directs it. Too much concentration blocks the natural flow of any psychic phenomena.

One exercise in Telepathy is to sit opposite a partner in a relaxed position. Designate one of you to be the "sender" and the other the "receiver." Now take a few deep breaths to clear your thinking. First the sender allows a thought or object to enter the mind and firmly but freely center on it, while the receiver remains open to any thoughts or images flowing through his or her mind. You can even add the factor of color to this exercise. The sender should envelope himself visually in the color red, while the receiver envisions the color blue. Holding hands or touching each other is not necessary; however, for beginners of Telepathy, this may stimulate the auric (see AURA) field between you. After only several minutes of using this technique, the receiver may pick up some portion of the message sent. As soon as the receiver feels ready to say what flows through the mind, do so aloud.

Recommended Reading

Bailey, Alice. *Telepathy and the Etheric Vehicle.* New York: Lucis Publishers, 1971. Many ideas about Telepathy and parapsychology in general.

Devereux, George, editor. *Psychoanalysis and the Occult.* San Francisco: University Press, 1970. Work looking at the connections between Telepathy and dreams.

Ehrenwald, Jan. *Telepathy: A Study of Telepathy in Interpersonal Relationships.* Salem, NH: Ayer Co. Publishers, 1975. A psychiatrist looks at psi phenomena.

Eisenbud, Jule, M.D. *Parapsychology and the Unconscious.* Berkeley: North Atlantic Books, 1983. A look at psi phenomena by a man said to have wed the philosophies of Buddha and Freud.

Puharich, A. *Beyond Telepathy.* New York: Anchor/Doubleday, 1973.

Rhine, L. *Hidden Channels of the Mind.* New York: W. Sloane Assoc., 1961. Case studies on Telepathy.

Targ, Russell, and Keith Harary. *The Mind Race.* New York: Villard Books, 1984. Understanding and using psychic ability.

Ullman, M., and Stanley Krippner. *Dream Telepathy, Second Edition.* Jefferson, NC: McFarland & Co. Inc., 1989. Telepathy and REM sleep.

Unidentified Flying Object (UFO)

An UNIDENTIFIED FLYING OBJECT/UFO is some-
thing seen in the sky of an unidentified origin (possibly
a flying craft from some place other than Earth).

In 1772 the French Academy appointed a committee to investigate continued reports of flaming objects (thought to be stones) streaking through the sky and crashing to the ground. After long deliberation and examination of the extensive evidence, they came to the conclusion that there were no such things as hot stones which fall from the sky because stones do not exist in the sky. Therefore, these reports were said to be "delusionary visions" with no basis in reality or simply stones thrown from volcanic eruptions and carried by the winds. Any other explanation for this phenomenon — now called "meteorites" — resulted in ridicule and harassment.

The UFO phenomenon is also a highly controversial riddle. However, visual sightings around the world by reputable witnesses; photographs and films pronounced "genuine" by competent experts; and the wealth of geographical, historical, exobiological, and meteorological evidence validating the existence of UFOs demands our serious consideration. We may never explain the UFO phenomenon completely, yet something clearly *real* continues to dart about in our atmosphere causing a preponderance of physical evidence and making it impossible to dismiss UFOs as mere "delusionary visions."

UFO landing sites are often scorched and radioactive with deep indentations in the ground. UFOs have been traced by both military and civilian radar and have been known to stop internal combustion engines and interfere with radio and television transmissions. Documented reports of radiational effects such as, eye inflammations, temporary blindness, shocks, burns, temporary paralysis, loss of consciousness, and various psychological effects have been experienced by persons who have had a UFO encounter.

Biologist and author, Lyall Watson, has studied the effects of UFOs on our feathered and furry friends, he writes:

Dogs, it seems, are the best UFO detectors, and dislike them
intensely. Some of them bark, some howl, some froth, and some
cower in terror when an object is about. It may be a high-

pitched sound which alerts them, or it may be microwave transmissions.... Many other species are equally unenthusiastic. Cats hiss and spit, sheep stampede, horses rear up, cows lie down, and birds simply stop singing. Most reactions seem to be temporary, but a few persist. Cattle refuse for several days to be herded into paddocks over which UFOs have been seen to hover; and in one case a single sniff at a recent landing site sent a dog dashing away howling.

Lawrence Fawcett and Barry Greenwood, authors of *Clear Intent*, state that United States military officials have known for four decades that UFOs do indeed exist; and furthermore, they exhibit technology advanced beyond our comprehension. Top military official, General George S. Brown, testified in 1974 before a Congressional Subcommittee, "They [UFOs] caused us a lot of trouble in Vietnam." Despite repeated denials by the United States Government, more than a few Air Force officials believe something is out there that cannot be written-off as swamp gas or weather balloons.

The abductee case of Betty and Barny Hill continues to offer data regarding extraterrestrial contact. After their abduction in 1964 by a UFO, Betty Hill drew a map of a three-dimensional holographic image of space that she saw aboard the alien craft. It was not until 1969, after an update of our astronomical data, that the information contained in the "Hill Star Map" was found to be accurate. Betty Hill's map drawn in 1964 included data unknown to anyone on Earth at the time! The home base of her abductors was calculated to be thirty-seven light years from Earth in the constellation Reticulum.

Whitley Strieber, a successful novelist, has recently authored two nonfiction books — *Communion* and *Transformation* — which are supposedly accounts of his frightening UFO contacts and abductions. Strieber conducted rigorous and incisive analysis backed by hard evidence. He sought out an eminent psychiatrist and a polygraph expert, both attesting to his sincerity. Strieber believes that a benevolent alien intelligence is "slowly coming into contact with us according to an agenda of their own devising, which proceeds as human understanding increases."

Extraterrestrial contact has been documented throughout human history. It is becoming glaringly apparent that we are not alone in our vast universe. Our Milky Way Galaxy contains more than 135 billion stars and there are more than 100 billion galaxies in the visible universe.

Isaac Asimov estimates the existence of at least 64 million Earth-like, life-bearing planets in our galaxy alone. Since our sun is a relatively young star, exobiological studies suggest that in the older star systems we would find more highly evolved and super-technological inhabitants.

UFOs seem to come in all shapes and sizes, singly or in groups, and travel at various speeds. There is often a whimsical flavor to UFO experiences which makes them difficult to take seriously. Many researchers believe UFOs are parapsychic — ethereal, reflecting light like ghosts. If they are parapsychical, they may primarily exist in another dimension that interpenetrates our spacetime. This might explain the so called "soft sightings" where UFOs seem to vanish and then suddenly reappear.

Celebrated psychologist and author Carl Jung proposed that the "reality status" of UFOs is more than psychological in nature but something less than solid. He believed that the archetypal symbol (see ARCHETYPAL SYMBOLS) of the flying saucer represents unity and wholeness, a healing female mandala. This may be why we see more UFOs during moments of great world stress or expansion.

Recommended Reading

Hall, Richard. *Uninvited Guests.* Sante Fe, NM: Aurora Press, 1988. A documented history of sightings and alien encounters.

Keel, John A. *Why UFOs?* New York: Manor Books, Inc., 1976. A para-psychic exploration and explanation.

Mufon UFO Network, Inc. *Mufon UFO Journal.* 103 Oldtown Road, Seguin, TX 78155-4099. Ufology Network and monthly Journal.

Sanderson, Ivan I. *Uninvited Visitors.* New York: A Cowles Book, 1967. A biologist's look at UFOs.

Story, Ronald D. *UFOs and the Limits of Science.* New York: Morrow & Co., 1981. A panel of experts study the ten most baffling UFO cases on record.

Strieber, Whitley. *Communion: A True Story.* New York: Avon Books, 1987.

Strieber, Whitley. *Transformation.* New York: Avon Books, 1988.

Vibrational Energy/Tonal Resonance

VIBRATIONAL ENERGY is the underpinning of all reality. The esoteric core of religious and mystical belief holds that we live in a "vibrating universe."

TONAL RESONANCE is the harmony between the Vibrational Energy of persons or things.

Poetry and science were blended with the observation that even a violin lying on a table hums gently to itself — as is true of all matter. The cosmos sings an oscillating song of jumbling wave lengths and dances to the beat of vibrating frequencies. The universe is all a chatter and full of noise. Although to the eye a piece of metal or a stone may seem passive and inert, it is actually a symphony of life and is filled with activity. In the *Tao of Physics*, Fritjof Capra writes:

...subatomic particles, then, are bundles of energy, or patterns of activity.... All objects are merely patterns in an inseparable cosmic process.

This is also the way in which the Eastern mystics see the material world. They emphasize that the universe has to be grasped dynamically, as it moves, vibrates and dances; that nature is not static, but a dynamic equilibrium.

Everything that exists — even thought, sight, color and music — vibrates in cycles at varying rates per second. Vibrations which emanate from the finger-tips and heal were once thought of as magic. Now our science has explained many types of vibrations and has invented useful ways to measure and use them, i.e., ultrasonics, X-rays, and lasers.

Vibrations appear to us as nonmaterial or as solid matter depending on their wavelength. Nevertheless, everything is basically vibration, movement, and frequency. Vibrations transmitted to our consciousness via the sense organs are perceived as matter, sound, heat, smell, light, taste. Higher nonmaterial frequencies, such as thought waves, are only discernible to us through our brain and nerve centers. Beyond this level are still higher frequency rays continuing up to the highest of all frequencies, the divine Creative Force.

The Tonal energy of a person or thing is the melody or voiceprint which identifies its particular frequency. This Tonal vibration originates from the auric (see AURA) or electromagnetic body. Its telltale nature can be sensed by one's unconscious or superconscious mind. What we cannot detect with the five senses we categorize and analyze through our personal intuitive "sonar." People often feel instances of immediate like or dislike toward the "vibes," or Tonal energy of another person without rational justification. When Tonal Resonance is experienced, a harmonious subtle energy level is expressed — a web of connectedness between people or things.

An interconnectedness or relationship exists between all energy in the cosmos and lies at the core of what is termed "vibrational empathy." This Vibrational empathy gives the very sensitive individual the ability to read auras, instigate healings, locate lost objects through psychometry (see PSYCHOMETRY), and other extra-sensory activities.

Recommended Reading

Davidson, John. *Subtle Energy.* Great Britain: Saffron Walden, 1987. Involved and interesting.

Fidler, J. Havelock. *Earth Energy.* Great Britain: The Aquarian Press, 1980. Earth's Vibrational Energy zones.

Gunther, Bernard. *Energy Ecstasy.* North Hollywood, CA: Newcastle Publishing Co., 1983.

Words of Substance

"Well, Richard, we're magnets, aren't we?... We're iron, wrapped in copper wire, and whenever we want to magnetize ourselves we can. Pour our inner voltage through the wire, we can attract whatever we want to attract...."

I ate a potato chip and frowned at him.

"You left out one thing. How do I do it?"

"You don't do anything. Cosmic law, remember? Like attracts like. Just be who you are, calm and clear and bright."

Richard Bach, *Illusions*

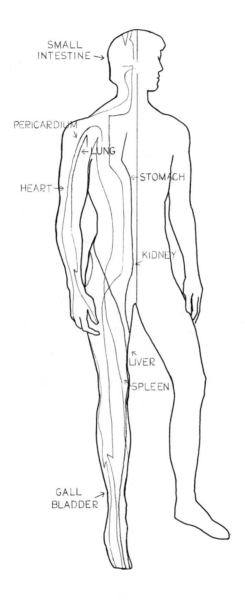

SMALL
INTESTINE →

PERICARDIUM

← LUNG

HEART →

← STOMACH

KIDNEY

LIVER

SPLEEN

GALL
BLADDER

Acupuncture/Acupressure

Acupuncture/Acupressure

ACUPUNCTURE is rooted in Chinese medicine developed over two thousand years ago. It employs the insertion of small sterile needles into the surface of the skin.

ACUPRESSURE, also from traditional Chinese medicine, is a type of bodywork therapy using energy-based pressure points.

Quoting Certified Acupuncturist, Stephanie Lum, "Acupuncture is a therapy used to prevent disease and maintain health. The practice consists of either stimulating or dispersing the flow of energy within the body by the insertion of needles into specific points on the surface of the skin."

These points are found in body pathways, or meridians, which contain life's energy called "chi." By the insertion of small needles into the top layers of the skin at these points, the practitioner gently twists them to balance or unblock the flow of energy within the body and thereby return it to proper health. Acupuncture has a positive effect of stimulating, or strengthening, the body's immune system.

Acupressure is the use of the balls of the thumb and fingers in much the same way as the needles are used in Acupuncture. The pressure is applied at the same points within the meridians to unblock the body's energy. These manipulation techniques can be incorporated into other types of bodywork or massage (see BODYWORK/MASSAGE) to ensure the total clearing of any blocks to life's vital energy flow. One type of massage called Shiatsu, strictly addresses the use of acupressure — Shiatsu literally means "finger pressure." This is a relaxing form of Acupressure which brings the entire body/mind into a situation of peaceful harmony.

Recommended Reading

Mann, Felix. *Acupuncture.* New York: Vintage Books-Random House, 1971. The ancient Chinese art of healing and how it works scientifically.

Seem, Mark. *Acupuncture Energetics.* Rochester, VT: Thorsons Publishers, Ltd. 1987. A workbook for diagnosis and treatment.

Suib-Cohen, Sherry. *The Magic of Touch.* New York: Harper & Row, 1987. An insightful handbook for therapeutic touch massage.

Teeguarden, Iona M. *The Joy of Feeling; Bodymind Acupressure.* Japan: Japan Publishing, Inc., 1987. Very in-depth instruction with pictures.

Biofeedback

BIOFEEDBACK (biological-feed-back) is a term used to describe a method of body/mind control when the body relays information back to you through various instruments regarding its status and functioning ability.

Approximately thirty years ago a new technique called Biofeedback was developed. It is a method in which one can learn to self-regulate bodily functions previously thought of as autonomic (automatic). This discovery shifts some of the responsibility for health from the health practitioner to the patient, as in the concepts of holistic medicine (see HOLISM/HOLISTIC HEALTH).

Some of the areas in which Biofeedback can be an aid are: heart rate, high blood pressure, headaches, muscle spasms, pain control, stress and tension, asthma, and many others, including some psychosomatic conditions. The principle behind Biofeedback is based on the "hot/cold" syndrome. Remember the child's game of hiding something and guiding another toward it with the shouting of "you're warm," "you're cold," "you're hot," until the treasure is reached? This principle also leads us to the biological reflex or response to hot and cold stimuli in Biofeedback.

Dr. John Mason puts it this way:

Monitoring devices provide a measure (a line on a graph, a blinking light, a buzzer, a tone) of autonomic, physiological functions. Through a series of trial and error alterations in behavior, you strive to maintain the desired reading. When you control the reading, you are also controlling the automatic process being monitored.

Clinical Biofeedback introduces a patient to the internal biological function, such as heart rate, then teaches the patient to actively regulate that function. It is important not to overemphasize the instruments being used, for then, Biofeedback would become only another "aspirin" to an undiscovered dis-ease. The ultimate goal of Biofeedback is to eventually remove the patient from the use of the instruments and allow the patient to control the symptoms through the mind-control techniques of imagery and visualization, self-hypnosis (see HYP-NOSIS/HYPNOTHERAPY), and relaxation techniques.

Recommended Reading

Brown, Barbara. *New Mind, New Body.* New York: Harper & Row, 1974. A useful look at the development of Biofeedback.

Danskin, David, and M. Crow. *Biofeedback: An Introduction and Guide.* Mountain View, CA: Mayfield Publishing Co., 1981. Concise overview.

Garder, Kenneth, and Penelope Montgomery. *Clinical Biofeedback: A Procedural Manual.* Maryland: Waverly Press, 1977.

Green, Elmer, and Alyce Green. *Beyond Biofeedback.* New York: Dell Publishing Co., 1977. Questions answered on how and why Biofeedback really works.

Mason, John L. *Guide to Stress Reduction.* Berkeley: Celestial Arts, 1985. Good overview of Biofeedback.

Norris, Patricia, and Garrett Porter. *I Choose Life: The Dynamics of Visualization and Biofeedback.* Walpole, NH: Stillpoint Publications, 1987.

Pelletier, Kenneth. *Holistic Medicine, From Stress to Optimum Health.* New York: Dell Publishing, 1979. A thorough look at holistic health today and the place of Biofeedback in clinical use.

For more information write to: The Biofeedback Society of America, 4301 Owens Street, Wheat Ridge, CO 80030.

Bodywork/Massage

BODYWORK and MASSAGE are forms of touch therapy. Many times used in conjunction with other modes of therapy, Bodywork and/or Massage can help alleviate stress and tension, release emotional blocks, balance the mind and body, and generally nourish the need for touch.

Numerous studies have been conducted which demonstrate the human need for touch. These studies indicate that without the fulfillment of this basic need, we would shrivel and ultimately die. Today there are many types of Bodywork and Massage therapies. Listed below are a few of the most popular along with a brief explanation of their style.

Feldenkrais: This Bodywork involves not only the body but also the brain. By instructing the body how to move in a more effective manner, the participant can retrain the body. These re-education classes are called "Awareness Through Movement" or ATM classes. In conjunction with movement, light touch Massage is used to guide the body to move in its most functional way. Breathing exercises are also employed to help align the total body/mind.

Rolfing: Rolfing is one of the more intense types of Bodywork employing a deep tissue manipulation to re-align the muscles. It is believed that the body, the deep muscles in particular, hold onto old patterns and traumas from the past. During a Rolfing session it is not unusual to experience some discomfort during manipulation which leads to an emotional release.

Shiatsu: Shiatsu is a meridian-based Massage originating from traditional types of acupressure (see ACUPUNCTURE/ACUPRESSURE). This type of Massage uses the thumb and balls of the fingers to transmit pressure to the energy points or meridians found throughout the body. It is a passive, relaxing type of Bodywork which enhances the balance of the total body frame.

Trager Integration: Tragering is a gentle Massage using rhythmic manipulations along with wide stretching movements. There is usually no deep pressure applied with this Bodywork, however, there is much movement of the limbs to establish rhythm and total body functioning.

Rocking, bouncing, stretching, and swinging is used to release gross body inhibitions.

Reichian: Reichian therapy is a powerful psychological Bodywork technique. This therapy employs various emotional releasing techniques such as: deep breathing; pounding and kicking with the feet; shaking the limbs; pushing on the chest; using convulsive reflex; and deep tissue Massage. The intent is to become aware of, and to release, repressed emotional energy to unblock suppressed emotional and psychological blockages.

There are many other types of traditional and holistic Massage and Bodywork techniques not mentioned here that can be located by writing or calling your local health or recreation center. Several of the books recommended below list the different types of Bodywork available today and how to select a practitioner.

Recommended Reading

Dull, Harold. *Bodywork Tantra: On Land and In Water.* Middletown, CA: Harbin Springs Publishing, 1987. Step-by-step instruction by the inventor of a unique form of bodywork done in the water.

Feldenkrais, Moshe. *Awareness Through Movement.* New York: Harper & Row, 1972. Details therapy.

Heller, Joseph, and William Henkin. *Bodywise.* Los Angeles: J.P. Tarcher, Inc., 1987. Examples and illustrations.

Kogan, Gerald. *Your Body Works.* Berkeley: And/Or Press, 1981. Provides overview articles covering several styles of Bodywork/Massage.

Miller, Barbara DeLong. *Psychic Massage.* New York: Harper & Row, 1975. Channeling the body's energy through Massage.

Smith, Fritz Frederick, M.D. *Inner Bridge.* Atlanta, GA: Humanics New Age, 1986. Explanation of movement and body.

Chiropractic

> *CHIROPRACTIC refers to a type of medical practice using the principles of holistic health. It is based in the belief that the body is capable of maintaining health through proper alignment of the nervous system by manipulations of the spine.*

Chiropractic medicine uses no drugs or chemicals. With its belief in a holistic approach to health, Chiropractic stands firm in the statement that "nature needs no help."

The techniques of Chiropractic care are to re-align any vertebrae along the spinal cord which have been pushed out of alignment by either physical traumas or emotional stress. When a subluxation (misalignment) occurs, a variety of manipulative techniques are employed to adjust the spinal column back to its proper place. The use of x-rays, heat, soundwave, bodywork/massage, and spinal manipulations are the primary tools of a Chiropractor.

One of the many documented cases of Chiropractic success is that of hearing restored to a person who was deaf for seventeen years. Chiropractic treatments to his cervical spine also relieved chronic pain and corrected various internal maladies. Chiropractic's premise of health and treating the whole person (mind, body, and spirit) succeeds in allowing an individual self-education, obtaining support services, and undergoing therapeutic treatment to maintain a total wellness regimen.

Recommended Reading

The Boston Women's Health Collective. *The New Our Bodies, Ourselves.* New York: Simon & Schuster, Inc., 1984. Brief overview on Chiropractic in a comprehensive book.

The Foundation for Chiropractic Education and Research. *Chiropractic Health Care.* Davenport, IA: 1979. Overview of history, pictures, and application.

The New Holistic Health Handbook. New York: Berkeley Holistic Health Center, 1985. Article by Dr. G.F. Riekeman on the basic principles of Chiropractic medicine.

Color Healing

*COLOR HEALING entails the use of various techni-
ques using direct or indirect color or color patterns.
It stems from a belief that the electromagnetic energy
emitted from all colors can be used in a curative
manner.*

The application of Color Healing, or more accurately
Chromotherapy, is directed toward re-establishing the balance of the
body's color energy system.   Chromotherapy dates back to ancient
Egypt and begins with the chakra system (see CHAKRA) which
becomes the seven doorways to color healing.   Each chakra center
possesses an aligning color vibration.   This nurturing, or restorative
factor, together with various methods is employed to regain a balance
of color intensity or vibrational pattern (see VIBRATIONAL ENER-
GY/TONAL RESONANCE).

One of the methods used in Chromotherapy is color breathing. This
technique is used in conjunction with visualization, or the imagining of
a color actually being breathed into the body. Another method employing visualization is to visualize a certain chakra center spinning its color
outward over the body.

Sometimes colored lamps or screens are used directly over the body
to infuse the healing light energy; or perhaps one might be asked to
drink solarized liquid from a particular colored glass or cup. All these
procedures can be used separately or in conjunction depending upon
the diagnosis and treatment given.   Chromotherapy serves to balance
the physical body's color energy (the effect) and the etheric, or auric
(see AURA) energy to reach the *cause* of the imbalance. Different
treatments or applications of color healing can correct imbalances,
ensuring health and attunement.

Color energy constantly affects us unknowingly in relation to:
What color we decide on to clothe our bodies; the color of the rooms
in which we choose to live and work; the color of the furniture we buy;
the color of the food we eat; and the colors in the natural environment
surrounding us. We cannot be where color is not touching us in some
way, even the sun's rays folding down upon us bring healing colors of

light. Ultraviolet and infrared rays from the sun are two of the invisible color rays sometimes used in color therapy to attain balance.

Within the visual rainbow of colors there are three *hot* colors (red, orange, yellow) and three *cold* colors (blue, indigo, violet). Green on the color scale becomes the balancing vibration found within the heart chakra and can be used for all types of healing. One can actually verify this fact of temperature difference between colors by simply filling two glasses with tap water. Put the same temperature water into a red glass and a blue glass. Place a thermometer in each of the glasses and witness the temperature difference. The water in the *red* glass will be warmer!

While undergoing an acupuncture (see ACUPUNCTURE/ ACUPRESSURE) treatment, one of the authors experienced the color energies swirl and spin over her body in a "gyroscope-like" manner. Visualize this description while lying prone with arms out-stretched. The red ray begins at the feet moving up to the point of chi energy (root chakra) and initiates the gyroscope while gently blending in the orange and yellow rays about six inches from the body. The green ray enters from the left hand flowing through the arms and integrates the heart center, forming the second circle. White light from the spiritual nature shoots directly down through the top to form the axis and grounding with the physical. The violet/indigo ray penetrates the head and streams into a gently humming ball in the center. Imagine yourself lying down with all the colors and energies spinning in different directions just above your chest and enjoy the healing.

Recommended Reading

Ballard, Juliet Brooke. *The Hidden Laws of Earth.* Virginia Beach, VA: A.R.E. Press, 1979. Color uses described by Edgar Cayce.

Don, Frank. *Color Magic.* Rochester, VT: Destiny Books, 1987. Learn to use personal color power.

Goodman, Linda. *Star Signs: The Secret Codes of the Universe.* New York: St. Martin's Press, NY, 1987. Many insights into the meaning of color and how to use it.

Haich, Elisabeth, and Reuben Amber. *Color Therapy.* New York: Aurora Press, 1983. Specific applications of color in all facets of life.

Hills, Christopher. *You Are a Rainbow.* Boulder Creek,CA: University of the Trees Press, 1979. Exact color charts for information about the energies behind the colors.

Hunt, Roland. *The Seven Keys to Colour Healing.* London: C.W. Daniel Co., 1973 (may be out of print). A complete outline of the practice of color therapy.

Crystal/Gem Healing

CRYSTAL AND GEM HEALING have been revived by the New Age healers of today. Healing techniques have been passed down through the centuries dating back as far as 400 B.C. We find evidence of Crystals and Gems being used for diagnosis and treatment throughout history.

Crystals and Gems are formed deep within the Earth's core. Pieces of dust particles within the layers of sediment deposit (magma) mixes with gases and water particles to form Earth's natural jewelry boxes. This process may take a few moments for some types and thousand of years for others. There are several divisions of Crystals and Gems based on factors such as geometric structure and molecular similarity.

Crystals and Gems have been worn for beauty, adored by royalty, used as generators in various modern items such as watches and computers, and of course, used for centuries as a healing source. Crystals and Gems work as reflectors or conductors of energy. If placed in a room with "negative vibrations," a crystal is said to lighten or clear away this negativity. Or, in the same way, if placed around or on the physical body, Crystals with their healing energies will transmute disease and inharmony into ease and balance.

In the suggested readings listed, you will find several "layouts" for healing the body, mind, and spirit. Working with healing stones is considered a serious responsibility by New Age healers and should be attempted only by those familiar and knowledgeable with their powers.

Some of these healing Crystals and Gems can be used in conjunction with the body's chakra system (see CHAKRA). By aligning the colors of the seven chakras with differently colored Crystals and Gems, it is thought that one can channel the positive pure light energy from the stone to the chakra center, therefore, dispelling any negativity found within that particular center. Many of these Crystals are found in just the right color, or color combinations, to adjust and balance these energy centers, as well as, the body's aura (see AURA).

Below is a partial list of healing stones which can be used in conjunction with the chakras:

First chakra - black tourmaline, smokey quartz, bloodstone, and garnet.

Second chakra - ruby, wulfenite, citrine, and amber.

Third chakra - orange citrine, yellow topaz, and calcite.

Fourth chakra - peridot, emerald, pink/green tourmaline, rhodochrocite, and rose quartz.

Fifth chakra - chrysocholla, turquoise, and aquamarine.

Sixth chakra - sodalite, lapis, sapphire, fluorite, sugelite, and amethyst.

Seventh chakra - clear quartz, diamond, selenite, and gold/white topaz.

Recommended Reading

Baer, Randall and Vicki. *The Crystal Connection and Windows of Light.* Los Angeles: Harper & Row, 1986. Two works exploring the energies of Crystals and their connection to personal and planetary evolution.

Kaplan, Miriam. *Crystals and Gemstones: Windows of the Self.* San Rafael, CA: Cassandra Press, 1987. A delightful guide.

Raphaell, Katrina. *Crystal Enlightenment.* New York: Aurora Press, 1985. Basic use of Crystals and Gems for healing.

Raphaell, Katrina. *Crystal Healing.* New York: Aurora Press, 1987. Many useful layouts for healing with Gems.

Sibley, Uma. *The Complete Crystal Guidebook.* California: U-Read Publishers, 1986. A practical path to self-development, empowerment, and healing through Crystals.

Earth's Energy Points/Power Spots

*The EARTH'S ENERGY POINTS/POWER SPOTS are
locations on our planet endowed with great energy or
force.*

The human body possesses pathways (or meridians) and points of life energy which are affected by the use of Acupuncture. Gaia, or "Mother Earth," is also theorized to be a single living system, a living body threaded with meridians and points of great vibratory intensity. It is believed that these amplified knots of magnetic energy on the Earth can be healing, conducive to abundant plant growth, influence one's connection with the Universal Mind, and enrich one's level of consciousness.

Power Spots on the Earth's surface discovered in ancient times are still honored as sacred. Stonehenge, Sedona, Mt. Sinai, the Bermuda Triangle, Findhorn, the Great Pyramids, and Mt. Shasta are said to be among the special geographical sites on Earth that emanate strength and power.

Recommended Reading

Barrow, John D., and Frank J. Tipler. *The Anthropic Cosmological Principle.* New York: Oxford University Press, 1988.

Merz, Blanche. *Points of Cosmic Energy.* Great Britain: Saffron Walden, 1987. Interesting information on Geobiology — the study of Earth's influence on living things at precise points on the Earth's surface.

Sutphen, Dick. *Sedona: Psychic Energy Vortexes.* Malibu, CA: Valley of the Sun Publishing, 1986.

Ecology/Stewardship

> *ECOLOGY is the study of plants and animals and their co-evolution with the Earth.*

> *STEWARDSHIP is the act of tending to, and caring for, the Earth.*

Minding the Earth, or Stewardship, is the focus of ecology today. This concept views the Earth and its natural resources as a bounty present for human use; *but* at the same time, enforces the act of Stewardship which demands re-cycling or re-storing our gifts from the Earth. Ecology arose from a conscious need to replenish that which is taken, for without this nurturing, our seemingly endless supply of oil, coal, timber, and minerals will vanish.

The public awareness of our environmental problems over the last few decades has brought Ecology to the forefront of our concerns. It is becoming obvious that issues such as nuclear waste, acid rain, global warming, ozone depletion, and the destruction of our oxygen-rich rain forests is threatening our survival. This needed publicity has helped us more fully comprehend (on an individual basis) why and how we can learn to co-exist with our planet Earth.

Gaia, Greek meaning "Earth Mother," is the name given to the Earth by James Lovelock, a chemist and inventor. This hypothesis suggests Earth is a living organism much like humankind with its own functions, eruptions, environmental controls, and ecological balances to preserve a constant state of equality or homogeneity.

Joseph Meeker, author and noted ecologist, writes, "Most likely the *Earth has a mind that also minds us,* so thinking often feels like a reciprocal exchange between familiars." The idea that the Earth is a "living organism" is not a new one. However, in this New Age (see NEW AGE) the concept of a living planet is emerging more and more readily with names, messages, correlations, and passages which describe our Earth in human languages. But as Dr. Meeker notes, "The best languages for a living Earth may not be verbal at all.... The languages of the Earth are eloquent *beyond words.*" It is appropriate to remember that our planet Earth, whether described as "a whole system," "Gaia," or "the Universal Mother," is our ticket to a new world:

Remember
that you are at an exceptional hour in a
unique epoch,
that you have this great happiness,
this invaluable privilege,
of being present at the birth of a new world.

Sri Aurobindo

Recommend Reading

Cornell, Joseph. *Listening to Nature.* Nevada City, CA: Dawn Publications, 1987. Pictorial account of our need for continued Ecology and Stewardship.

Deval, Bill, and George Sessions. *Deep Ecology: Living as if Nature Mattered.* Layton, UT: Gibbs Smith Publisher, 1985. Offering direct action suggestions.

The Earthworks Group. *50 Simple Things You Can Do To Save the Earth.* California: Earthworks Press, 1989.

The Findhorn Community. *The Findhorn Garden.* New York: Harper & Row, 1975.

Lovelock, James. *Gaia: A New Look at Life.* New York: Oxford University Press, 1979. Looking at the "Gaia Hypothesis" and Earth as a living organism.

McDonagh, Sean. *To Care for the Earth: A Call to a New Theology.* Santa Fe: Bear & Co., 1987. A healing vision of renewed Stewardship.

Meeker, Joseph W. *Minding the Earth.* California: The Latham Foundation, 1988. Small book about positive changes for tending to our Earth.

Russell, Peter. *The Global Brain.* Los Angeles: J.P. Tarcher, Inc., 1983. "An exploration of humanity's role and potential as it might be seen through the eyes of the planet."

Herbal Therapy

HERBAL THERAPY is the combining of various natural herbs, plants, barks and roots specified for healing the body/mind.

The use of herbs in a healing capacity brings us to a "re-discovery of our roots." Herbalism, or Herbal Therapy, dates back to the beginning of humanity. Early tribes are noted for their use of herbs as a source of healing; also, the ancient Egyptians utilized herbal healing (some were even found in King Tut's tomb). And, of course, the Chinese and Native American Indians base their healing techniques on the use of herbs and the natural elements of the Earth. The unity of Earth and humankind is the basis of the unique success of herbal healing.

Herbs are used in different methods or fashions for specific illnesses or to maintain balance. An herbalist may ask his patient to drink a mixture of herbs in a tea form. (It is important to remember not to use any aluminum or other toxic metal when steeping herb teas.) Another method of using herbs is in the form of a concentrated tincture. One may even be asked to bathe in a formula of herbal bath water or to wrap an area of the body in a pack filled with healing roots.

Herbs remind us of nature's own cyclic patterns. In Chinese medicine one main cause of illness is the resistance or inability to *change*. This inflexibility leads to an imbalance of the total system. It is said that anything which impairs the smooth flow of the life force in nature leads to disease. It is most important to flow with life's changes as nature teaches us so aptly. Through the study of Herbal Therapy and its relation to mother Earth, we begin to understand the healing cycles of nature.

Herbal Therapy is one of the avenues of holistic medicine (see HOLISM/HOLISTIC HEALTH) being re-discovered in this awakening New Age of unity with our planet. We have been given the natural tools for implementing health and wholeness in body, mind, and spirit if we but open ourselves to the natural wonders of Earth's abundance.

Recommended Reading

Gerber, Richard, MD. *Vibrational Medicine: New Choices for Healing Ourselves.* Santa Fe: Bear & Co., 1988. Energetic medicine covering Herbal Therapy, psychic healing, and other landmark disciplines.

Hoffman, David. *Successful Stress Control: The Natural Way.* London: Thorsons Publishers, Inc., 1987. U.S. Distributor: Samuel Weiser, York Beach, ME. In-depth study of Herbalism listing many herbal preparations.

Hyatt, Richard. *Chinese Herbal Medicine.* London: Thorsons Publishers, Inc., 1984. U.S. Distributor: Samuel Weiser, York Beach, ME.

Reilly, Harold J., and Ruth Hagy Brod. *The Edgar Cayce Handbook for Health Through Drugless Therapy.* New York: Jove Publications, Inc., 1979. Cayce's methods of Herbal Therapy given to thousands during his lifetime.

Holism/Holistic Health

Holism/Holistic Health

> *HOLISM is the integration of all parts with the whole. In the area of health, Holistic practices refer to the integration of physical, mental, and spiritual aspects to form a healthy whole being.*

Holistic Health is directed toward achieving perfect well-being in all aspects of life to support and maintain a feeling of ease, rather than dis-ease. Disease occurs when a portion of either body, mind, or spirit is undernourished. Because all three are critical to total well-being, a Holistic medical practitioner may prescribe family or individual counseling, meditation techniques, visualization, affirmations, specific physical activities, exercises or massage, hydrotherapy, vitamins, herbs, a special diet, or a combination of several such treatments.

Based on the principle that the body, mind, and spirit all contribute to wholeness, what affects one aspect of this trinity inevitably affects the others. Therefore, when the physical body is working at its optimum, the mind and spiritual natures benefit accordingly. When the mind is healthy, the spiritual and physical aspects tend to be healthy. A healthy mental attitude requires a positive creative mind aligned with constructive personal life goals. Advocates of Holistic Health use a variety of healing methods.

To pursue the Holistic approach to health and well-being the spiritual nature must also be considered. According to Harold Bloomfield, M.D., a Holistic Health advocate, people who are spiritually healthy and who have a sense of meaning or purpose in their lives are less likely to fall ill; and if they do, are more likely to recover quickly.

Taking responsibility for one's own wellness is the active ingredient in Holism. Applied Holistic principles can help one achieve and maintain optimum balance and integration of body, mind, and spirit for a whole healthy person.

Recommended Reading

Berkeley Holistic Health Center. *The New Holistic Health Handbook —Living Well in a New Age.* Lexington, MA: The Stephen Greene Press, 1985. A comprehensive guide to New Age health.

Bethards, Betty. *Techniques for Health & Wholeness: Healing of Body, Mind, and Spirit.* California: Inner Light Foundation, 1979.

Brenner, Paul. *Health is a Question of Balance.* Marina Del Rey, CA: DeVorss & Co., 1978. Inspirational.

Carlson, Richard, and Benjamin Shield, editors. *Healers on Healing.* Los Angeles: J.P. Tarcher, Inc., 1989. Anthology by renowned health professionals.

Cousins, Norman. *Anatomy of an Illness.* New York: W.W. Norton, 1979.

Dossey, Larry. *Space, Time, and Medicine.* Boston: Shambhala Publications, 1982. A view into the medical model of today and the Holistic paradigm of tomorrow.

Joy, Brugh. *Joy's Way.* Los Angeles: J.P. Tarcher, Inc., 1979.

Pelletier, Kenneth. *Holistic Medicine.* New York: Dell Publishing, 1979. Philosophy of a changing medical system in the New Age.

Pelletier, Kenneth. *Mind as Healer, Mind as Slayer.* New York: Delta Press, 1977.

Shealy, Noran, and Caroline Myss. *Breaking Through Illness: Igniting the Healing Power Within.* Walpole, NH: Stillpoint Publishing, 1988. Three cassette tapes and guidebook for healing the whole-self.

Iridology

> *IRIDOLOGY is the study and diagnosis of illness through evaluation of the human iris, the colored part of the eye.*

This system of medical diagnosis was developed in Western civilization over one hundred years ago and is being expanded by practitioners of the New Age medical paradigm (see PARADIGM SHIFT). It has been said that the eyes are the "windows of the soul;" they mediate the outer light of the sun and the inner light of the soul. How true this becomes when we observe the art of Iridology.

Iridology charts show to the exact point where each organ and/or system found in the body can be located inside the iris. These divisions reveal the relationship between the inner and outer portions of the body. With this knowledge, the practitioner can denote where in the body there is disease or imbalance. There are many signs or stages to look for within the iris itself, such as inflammation, flakes, clouds, density, color, fibers, spokes, nerve rings, and pigmentation.

In viewing an Iridology diagnosis chart it looks like a wheel with spokes and a hub. Each division pinpoints an exact part of the physical body to the iris. Depending upon the simple examination of the eye an accurate diagnosis for imbalances between systems is made. This method is non-invasive, bringing the entire body structure into view and can be readily used in conjunction with other methods of diagnosis.

Recommended Reading

Hall, Dorothy. *Iridology.* New Canaan, CT: Keats Publishing Inc., 1980. Contains many valuable pictures and information.

Jensen, Bernard. *The Science and Practice of Iridology.* California: Bernard Jensen, 1952. Complete history and practice of Iridology.

Lindlahr, Theodore. *Fundamental Basis of Iris Diagnosis.* London: Theodore Lindlahr, 1969. Basics in Iridology.

Wolf, Harri. *Applied Iridology.* California: Harri Wolf, 1979.

Rebirthing

> *REBIRTHING is an emotional release counseling technique with the purpose of helping one remember and re-experience the actual trauma of birth.*

The Rebirthing technique is a form of prana yoga (see YOGA) which employs a scientific rhythmic breathing with spiritual breathwork. Leonard Orr, the originator of the Rebirthing process feels it is a relaxed, connected breathing where the inhale is directly connected to the exhale and the inner breath merges with the outer. This merging of air sends vibrations through the nervous and circulatory systems which cleans and balances the human aura and body/mind.

The purpose of the Rebirthing process is to remember one's birth, to relive it physiologically, psychologically, and spiritually. Once this is accomplished, any emotional trauma associated with the birth process is released. The use of breathwork is employed to unravel the experience and acts as a relaxing tool to calm and cleanse the body/mind. The rebirthing session may last one hour or longer; however, the lesson is to connect the inhale to the exhale in a relaxed continuous rhythm.

Recommended Reading

Orr, Leonard. *Physical Immortality.* Berkeley: Celestial Arts, 1981. The Rebirthing process taken to the level of ancient teachings.

Orr, Leonard, and Sondra Ray. *Rebirthing in the New Age.* Berkeley: Celestial Arts, 1983. Complete description of the process of Rebirthing.

For a list of Rebirthing Centers near you write to: Rebirth America, P.O. Box 234, Sierraville, CA 96126. (916) 994-3552or (916) 994-3424.

Reflexology

REFLEXOLOGY is the system of applying pressure to reflex points, primarily to the feet and hands, which stimulates nerve endings and/or energy meridians.

As in acupuncture and acupressure, (see ACUPUNCTURE/ ACUPRESSURE) Reflexology entails the use of energy meridians as found in ancient Chinese medicine. In their article, "Reflexology," found in *The New Holistic Health Handbook,* Lew Connor and Linda McKim state, "Each zone has its own nerve-stimulation pattern, so that when a pressure is applied at a reflex point in that zone, a stimulation is sent to a corresponding organ or gland in that zone."

Reflexology assists in relaxation and unblocking nerve endings to help the parallel organs attain optimum functioning. This is a pleasant type of foot or hand massage which can be enjoyed by all age groups. You can easily give excellent Reflexology treatments to yourself and reap its unwinding and relaxing benefits.

Recommended Reading

Berkeley Holistic Health Center. *The New Holistic Health Handbook.* Lexington, MA: The Stephen Greene Press, 1985. Gives a complete look at how to give Reflexology treatments.

Berkson, Devaki. *The Foot Book: Healing with the Integrated Treatment of Foot Reflexology.* New York: Funk & Wagnalls, 1977.

Carter, Mildred. *Helping Yourself with Foot Reflexology.* New Jersey: Parker Publishing Co., 1969.

Stress Management

STRESS MANAGEMENT is a term given to a variety of techniques, tools, and exercises which help alleviate daily pressures and tensions that are labeled stress.

To look at the management of stress, we need to first define it. Stress has become a somewhat negative sounding word to our ears; however, without stress we could not even sit erect in our chairs while reading this material. Stress is a *resistance to* some thing, i.e., person, idea, emotion, fear, and so on. This resistance can be healthy, such as the opposing force of different muscles on the skeletal system to ensure our body's erect posture and movement, or the instinctual response of our mind and body to resist danger or harm which could cause us distress. At the same time, resistance can be unhealthy as in not acknowledging an emotion or fear held within that manifests in illness, or our resistance toward change and its inevitable affect on the balance of mind, body, and spirit. Therefore, healthy stress awareness is a positive and necessary part of our well-being. What is of concern is when the level of stress, instigated by either a healthy or unhealthy resistance, becomes unmanageable.

The stress response is a natural occurrence of living. The physical body does not care how or why you engage in a tension-producing situation, it responds exactly the same whether you are falling in love or being fired from your job. Messages from your brain are sent to all parts of the body in the form of nerve impulses, rapid breathing and heart rate, the secretion of extra hormones and other body/mind responses that indicate stress induction. What becomes important in the management of stress is staying aware, or conscious, of when and to what degree you are undergoing stressful symptoms.

All of us respond or react differently in potentially stressful situations. While extremely loud noises, such as disco music, may induce tension for some, it may be a calming agent for others. It is useful to understand our own healthy and unhealthy stress responses then we can create a "personal mental stress catalogue" for our individual use. To help facilitate this proposal, below is a list of potentially stressful (or even distressful) events which could happen in your life. Go down the list placing a mental check beside those experienced within the last year. The number of marks indicate degrees of stress.

LIFE EVENTS

Marriage
Divorce
Death of a spouse or family member
Separation
Detention in an institution
Major personal injury or illness
Loss of a job
Retirement
Pregnancy
Sexual difficulties
New family member through birth or adoption
Major changes in finances, for better or worse
Death of close friend
Change in employment or vocation
Child leaving home
In-law troubles
Outstanding personal achievement
Beginning a new love relationship
Change in personal habits — smoking, dieting, etc.
Move in residency
Taking a vacation
Change in working hours or conditions
Christmas or other important holiday

Now, to help you control or alleviate any extremely stressful responses to the list, test the techniques and tools used in Stress Management. These methods are divided into three categories: Physical or Body Oriented; Psychological or Mind Control; and Spiritual Awareness. Different aspects of all three categories can be employed for a balanced program of Stress Management.

Looking to the body, we find several tools to help alleviate stress:

Touch/Massage —relieves muscle constriction
Breath work — restores balanced oxygen supply
Diet/Nutrition —eliminating stimulants and eating a
*   balanced diet.*

Physical Exercise —walking, swimming, running, etc.
Yoga/Stretching —balances both mind and body
Vitamin & Herbal therapy —regain depleted nutrients
Progressive Relaxation —attunes body awareness
Biofeedback —mind/body control of nerves, muscles
Hydrotherapy —relaxes and reduces aches and
    soreness
Hugging —good old-fashioned Stress Management

To ensure a healthy mental attitude and balance the mind/body principle try:

Counseling/Psychotherapy —talking it out
Support Groups —get needed supportive feedback
Self-hypnosis/Hypnotherapy —reprogram
    subconscious mind
Desensitization —change reactions to world and life
Visualization —healing and re-programming the mind
Affirmation —positive statements of harmony
Autogenics —behavior change with mind control
Goal-setting —testing positive future outlook
Laughter —to lighten the mind

Lastly, but most importantly, consider your spiritual nature. Stress is initiated by the MIND, manifested in the BODY, but can be controlled or alleviated through the SPIRIT.

Join a local religious or spiritual group —social contact
    and support
Meditation —spiritual connection with the Universe
Automatic Writing —relieves stored energy, allows
    communication with Universal Mind
Praying —asking for guidance and direction
Channeling —answers from a higher power
Reading spiritual literature —education and calming
    affect on the mind, body, and spirit
Creativity —creating art brings spiritual forces to
    physical world
Yogic Mantras —calming sense of peace
Faith/Trust —believing in miracles and Divine Order

(Check Table of Contents or Index for detailed information on the previous Individual Headings.)

Choosing several of the above methods from the three groups will guide you on your way to a life with less unhealthy stress. Investigate and have *fun* with these new techniques — allow yourself to flow with life's changes.

Recommended Reading

Benson, Herbert, M.D. *Beyond the Relaxation Response.* New York: Times Books, 1984. The theory and practical uses of relaxation and mind control techniques.

Charlesworth, Edward A., and Ronald G. Nathan. *Stress Management.* New York: Ballantine Books, 1984. An in-depth look at stress and its relation to wellness.

Gawain, Shakti. *Creative Visualization.* New York: Bantam Books, 1982. Both works contain many guided visualizations and meditative exercises.

Gawain, Shakti. *Living in the Light.* San Rafael, CA: Whatever Publishing, Inc., 1986.

Hoffman, David. *Successful Stress Control: The Natural Way.* London (Dist. by Samuel Weiser, York Beach, ME): Thorsons Publishers, Inc., 1987. A look at what stress is and what it does, and healing it with herbs.

Mason, L. John. *Guide to Stress Reduction.* Berkeley: Celestial Arts, 1985. Manual with visualizations, progressive relaxation, meditation, and autogenics.

Pelletier, Kenneth. *Healthy People in Unhealthy Places.* New York: Delacorte Press/Seymour Lawrence, 1987. A look at the "burn-out syndrome."

Pelletier, Kenneth. *Mind as Healer, Mind as Slayer: A Holistic Approach to Preventing Stress Disorders.* New York: Dell Publishing Co., 1977. Detailed approach to medical therapy of Stress Management.

Touch Healing

> TOUCH HEALING is the process of "laying on of hands" used by physicians, nurses, therapists, spiritual counselors, and any person who understands the intense value of the act of touching another person.

The art of touching has been researched and studied for many decades in the Holistic Health (see HOLISM/HOLISTIC HEALTH) movement. Everyone — infant, child, adolescent, adult, and maturing adult — needs to be touched. We all gravitate toward this dimension of human nurturing and its source is not as important as the act itself.

"Laying on of hands" is a term used by practitioners who use this touching technique to "heal." To them touch is more than physical intimacy and comfort; it becomes a transmission of energy through one being to another. This "energy" is the cosmic force that binds all living and nonliving matter together. One can actually feel this energy between objects. Try this test. Rub your hands together, fast. This will activate the cosmic energy between your own hands. Now, gently and slowly pull your hands apart noting the polarities or resistances and simultaneously the magnetic energies stimulated as you are pulling your hands apart. Now, take one hand and sway it back and forth, up and down, from the other hand about three to five inches apart. Feel the resistance to clasp them together again? You are actually feeling the vibrational energy that is used in touch healing.

We are all healers and we can make ourselves open channels for the healing life energy through this laying on of hands technique. Many practitioners, as well as ordinary caring people, have learned the true value and healing qualities of the act of touching. Hospitals and clinics are beginning to employ this kind of healing on their patients with winning results.

The well-known Olga Worrall possessed great healing powers in her hands and shared her talent with many hundreds of people. Through her teachings many physicians learned the meaning of Touch Healing and where this phenomenon originated. She taught that the healing came from "a universal field of energy which is common to all creation. It stems from God, the universal source of all intelligence and power." In her biography, *Olga Worrall: Mystic with the Healing Hands* written by Edwina Cerutti, it is said that the "healees" of Olga's Touch Healing experienced an unusual degree of heat coming from her hands. Others said they felt a small electrical charge or shock. Olga's husband calls this healing energy "para-electricity" — meaning it comes from beyond (para) the electrical properties now known to humans.

One of the authors had the honor of meeting and experiencing the healing energy from Olga — it was a warm spiritual event. We would like to christen this healing energy that emits from each of us as "love current," for it is out of our love nature that touch brings healing.

Recommended Reading

Burns, Echo Bodine. *Touch Healing: Hands That Heal.* San Diego, CA: ACS Publishing, Inc., 1987. A spiritual healer shares insights on her own use of Touch Healing.

Gordon, Richard. *Your Healing Hands.* Berkeley: Wingbow Press, 1984. Pictorial book for the whole family.

Krieger, Dolores. *The Therapeutic Touch.* New York: Prentice-Hall, Inc., 1979. Work from the originator of Touch Healing.

Krippner, Stanley, and Alberto Villoldo. *The Realms of Healing, Third Edition.* Berkeley: Celestial Arts, 1986. A look at healers and healing methods.

Montagu, Ashley. *Touching.* New York: Harper & Row, 1986. Stimulating facts and analysis on touch.

Ponder, Catherine. *The Healing Secret of the Ages and The Dynamic Laws of Healing.* New York: Parker Publishing, 1967 and DeVorss & Co., 1966.

Worrall, Ambrose A. with Olga N. Worrall. *The Gift of Healing: A Personal Story of Spiritual Therapy, Second Edition.* Tustin, CA: Ariel Press, 1985.

Vegetarianism

> *VEGETARIANISM is comprised of three main variations: 1) Total Vegetarianism is a dietary exclusion of all but plant foods, 2) Lacto- Vegetarianism, relies on plant food plus dairy products, 3) Lacto-ovo-Vegetarianism utilizes plant foods plus eggs and dairy products. The term "vegetarian" came into general use with the formation of the Vegetarian Society of England in 1847.*

People state several different reasons for becoming a Vegetarian. Some say meat is heavy and difficult to digest — they feel lighter, healthier, and possess greater energy on a Vegetarian diet. Others recognize that by getting off the "top of the food chain," they consume far less pesticide residues. A growing percentage of Vegetarians see their meatless diet as a form of boycott against the abuses of modern animal farming, while others detest the killing of animals in general and choose to eat organisms with a lower evolutionary consciousness.

It is possible to meet all nutritional requirements on a Vegetarian diet, although it is recommended that one obtain appropriate information and guidelines before becoming a strict Vegetarian. A long list of successful athletes swear by their Vegetarian diet as the reason for their marvelous physical endurance. Leo Tolstoy, Leonardo da Vinci, George Bernard Shaw, and Gandhi are a few of the more notable Vegetarians who lived long creative lives.

Peter Singer, author of *Animal Liberation*, believes that it is unethical to inflict gross suffering on "nonhuman animals" by rearing them through intensive farming methods and then killing them simply to satisfy our taste buds. Ending world hunger is another argument Singer states for a Vegetarian revolution. He explains that, "...it takes twenty-one pounds of protein fed to a calf to produce a single pound of animal protein for humans. We get back less than five percent of what we put in."

This waste of food source is substantiated by former U.S. Assistant Secretary of Agriculture, Don Paarlberg. He reported that reducing livestock population by half in the United States alone "would make available enough food to make up the calorie deficit of the nonsocialist underdeveloped nations *nearly four times over.*"

There are many moral and health arguments for a Vegetarian diet or at least a decrease in the amount of meat we consume. Perhaps what is most important in the Vegetarian versus non-Vegetarian debate is that we are *conscious* about our food choices. We can learn from the American Indian tradition of our past. These people included meat in their diets, however, great reverence was expressed for the spirit of anything sacrificed for their consumption. They would have been appalled at our present day fast-food attitude and lack of respect for life.

Recommended Reading

Ballentine, Rudolph M., M.D. *Transition to Vegetarianism: An Evolutionary Step.* Honesdale, PA: Himalayan Publishers, 1987. An up-to-date compilation on the facts of Vegetarianism.

Robbins, John. *Diet for a New America.* Walpole, NH: Stillpoint Publishing, 1987. "How your food choices affect your health, happiness and the future of life on Earth."

Shulman, Martha Rose. *Gourmet Vegetarian Feasts.* Rochester, VT: Destiny Books, Inner Traditions, 1987. Vegetarian meals that draw rave reviews.

Singer, Peter. *Animal Liberation: A New Ethics for Our Treatment of Animals.* New York: Avon, 1975. A powerful experience filled with food for thought.

The Past Reborn

"Did you have the whole show, like you see in movies from India? Crowds in the streets, billions of hands touching you, flowers and incense, golden platforms with silver tapestries for you to stand on when you spoke?"

"No. Even before I asked for the job, I knew I couldn't stand that. So I chose the United States, and I just got the crowds."

Richard Bach, *Illusions*

Alchemy

> *ALCHEMY is the science of transformation. The alchemical transmutation of lead into gold was analogous to the purification of man into something more perfect.*

Alchemy flourished for over two thousand years until 1661. Its followers included such devotees as Paracelsus, Roger Bacon, Ben Johnson, John Dee, Thomas Aquinas, and Isaac Newton. Noted author and psychologist Carl Jung spent ten years studying the archetypal-rich material of the alchemical treatises and considered Alchemy a predecessor more to modern psychology than to modern chemistry. Jung dedicated four of his collected works to his belief that the alchemists' concerns were primarily the spiritual transformation (see TRANSFORMATION/TRANSCENDENCE) of dense physical matter.

Some authorities believe the word, "alchemy," was derived from the Arabic word, *al-kimiya* which is based on *khemia* — the Greek name for Egypt, meaning "the art of the black earth." An alternative derivation relates it to the Greek word, *khumos* — "chyme" or "juice," providing a connection to chemistry.

In an essay written for *The Laughing Man* magazine, Ralph Metzner explores the origins of Alchemy:

> *The Hermetic alchemical philosophers interacted vigorously with and contributed to the development of Christian theology and mysticism. For devout Christians, including many alchemists, the search for the philosophers' stone, or tincture of immortality, became synonymous with the quest for union with Christ.*

Medieval alchemists approached material reality as a vast, responsive, living entity. They were magician-healers and believed that matter could be purified through extraction of impure elements in one's consciousness. The chemical metaphor was used to symbolize this mental transformation — heavy, dark *lead* becoming pure, reflective *gold* was an ancient healing image. Outwardly, the interest of Alchemy appeared to be the mere mundane transmutation of metals, however, the inward focus was actually a devotional system of cooperation with nature as the key to spiritual evolution.

Recommended Reading

de Rola, Stanislas Klossowski. *Alchemy.* Great Britain: Thames & Hudson, Ltd, 1985. Historical study of Alchemy with authentic hermetic illustrations.

Jung, C.G. *Alchemical Studies.* Princeton, NJ: Princeton University Press, 1983. Five essays by Jung.

Metzner, Ralph. *Maps of Consciousness.* New York: The Macmillan Co., 1972. Wonderful section on Alchemy as the "Chemistry of Inner Union."

Von Franz, Marie-Louise. *Alchemical Active Imagination.* Dallas, TX: Spring Publications, Inc., 1979. Alchemy as a therapy of the soul.

Archetypal Symbols

Archetypal Symbols

> ARCHETYPAL SYMBOLS are patterns of instinctual behavior and racial memories that have been etched into our psyche through the endless repetition of human experience.

In 1919, famed psychologist Carl Jung theorized that within the collective unconscious (see COLLECTIVE UNCONSCIOUS) were certain "archaic remnants" and "primordial images" which he called archetypes. Archetypal situations include heroic struggles, birth, death, marriage, mother and father, *ad infinitum*. They touch a common chord of our heritage and originate from humanity's dreams, religious visions, fairy tales, and myths. Ancient mythology and the Greek tragedies, as well as modern plays, are often flavored by Archetypal Symbols and themes of conflict and relationship.

When we reach deep within the collective unconscious to this Archetypal layer, we become energized by the distant yet familiar memory of these images. We can incorporate this new understanding into our personal experience by translating their meanings. For example, the "wise old man," "Earth Mother" or "sage" are archetypes most often representative of what we call our Higher-Self (see HIGHER-SELF), spirit guide, or God-Self. The surfacing of this omniscient image to one's conscious awareness — whether through a dream, art, myth, religious vision, or meditative practices — may bring with it an influx of powerful transformative energy or be a comforting message of connectedness and protection.

Recommended Readings

Campbell, Joseph. *The Hero with a Thousand Faces.* Princeton, NJ: Princeton University Press, 1949. One of Campbell's most well-known and beloved works.

Jung, C.G. *The Archetypes and the Collective Unconscious.* Princeton, NJ: Princeton University Press, 1980. Pure, brilliant Jung.

Jung, C.G. *Four Archetypes.* Princeton, NJ: Princeton University Press, 1973.

Astrology

> *ASTROLOGY is the study of the positions of the planets in our solar system and their influences on human affairs. Each of the ten major planets (with the sun and moon) possess a distinctly different set of influences upon one's life. Astrology attempts to interpret those effects on the individual to maximize self-realization and a "quality of being."*

The Chaldeans of Babylonia are credited with developing the practice of Astrology in 3000 B.C. Early Greek, Egyptian, Hindu, and Chinese cultures have each contributed to modern understanding of the relationships between the planets, their angles to each other and to the Earth at the precise moment of a person's birth, and their combined influence on human character or personality.

Planetary positions at birth are illustrated by means of a horoscope, or natal chart resembling a wheel with twelve spokes. Its interpretation requires understanding the influence of each of the planets and their "aspects" or positions relative to one another, the signs, the characteristics of the twelve signs of the zodiac (the division of the heavens), and the properties of each of the twelve "houses" or pie-shaped sections of the chart which refer to certain areas of life.

In addition to the charted planets, signs, and houses, a horoscope determines one's rising sign or ascendant, the constellation of the zodiac rising on the eastern horizon at the exact moment of birth. Jeanne Avery explains the ascendant's significance in her book, *The Rising Sign*: "[It] is a person's own particular 'horizon' or point of view....indicative of the personality of the individual."

To study Astrology is to study all aspects of human nature, to gain insight and sensitivity to how we are likely to react given a particular set of circumstances. It is a process that encourages self-discovery and plays a role in individual destiny.

Influences and effects of the planets:

Sun - The Sun influences one's physical appearance and nature or psychology as it expresses itself outwardly. The Sun is considered the masculine energy of your horoscope.

Moon - The Moon rules intuition, hunches or instincts, and the heart's desires. Inner creative work such as art, writing and music are affected by the Moon's sign, as is love and nurturing. The Moon represents the feminine nature.

Mercury - Mercury influences one's reactions to impressions (sight, sound, odor, taste, and touch), as well as one's communicatory abilities. Mercury is called the planet of intellectual movement and of progress. Its qualities are attentiveness, excitability, impressionability, and a tendency to worry.

Venus - Venus influences sexuality and emotional nature and is associated with harmony in love and peace. Venus affects one's sympathy, pleasures, balance, and fair judgment.

Mars - This planet determines the channels through which the physical, mental, and spiritual energies will most easily and naturally flow. It expresses itself in one's actions, assertiveness, strength, inventiveness and creativity.

Jupiter - Jupiter is the planet of luck, both good and bad. It influences opportunity and the desire to experience life at its fullest. Jupiter is representative of personal growth and the expansion of intellect and moral character.

Saturn - Saturn influences self-preservation, one's method of defense, or way of dealing with reality and the world. This planet governs organization, concentration, responsibility, ambition, and stability.

Uranus - Uranus is the planet that affects the desire for personal freedom and individualism. Its influence is often experienced as jolting changes that occur throughout life. Uranus also rules insight and intuitive knowledge.

Neptune - Neptune influences the subconscious, inherited traits and mentality, as well as psychic ability, mediumistic power, and prophecy.

Pluto - Pluto's affect is regenerative, symbolizing both death and rebirth. It influences transformation, decay and resurgence.

Characteristics of the twelve zodiac signs, or sun signs:

Aries - dynamic, zestful, pioneering, active, independent.

Taurus - steady, grounded, conservative, practical, generous.

Gemini - dual-natured, restless, mental, fun-loving, creative.

Cancer - nurturing, giving, stubborn, spend-thrift, intuitive.

Leo - dramatic, outgoing, lover, regal, self-pride, vital.

Virgo - discriminating, detail-oriented, planner, analytical.

Libra - balance, grace, indecisiveness, romantic, diplomatic.

Scorpio - passionate, transformative, secretive, imaginative.

Sagittarius - free-flowing, comical, idealistic, philosophic.

Capricorn - steadfast, organizational, ambitious, leadership.

Aquarius - altruistic, inventive, scattered, humanitarian.

Pisces - emotional, psychic, harmonious, encompassing.

Recommended Reading

Avery, Jeanne. *The Rising Sign.* New York: Doubleday/Dolphin Books, Inc., 1982. Detailed interpretations.

Goodman, Linda. *Linda Goodman's Star Signs.* New York: St. Martin's Press, 1988. Also by Linda Goodman, *Sun Signs and Love Signs.* Bantam Books, NY, 1986 and Fawcett, NY, 1978.

Swami Kriyananda. *Your Sun Sign as a Spiritual Guide.* Nevada City,CA: Ananda Publishing, 1979. Captures the spiritual dimension.

Lewi, Grant. *Astrology for the Millions.* St. Paul, MN: Llewellyn Publications, 1975. A favorite standby.

River, Lindsay, and Sally Gillespie. *The Knot of Time: Astrology and the Female Experience.* New York: Harper & Row, 1987.

Sakoian, Frances, and Louis S. Acker. *The Astrologer's Handbook,* New York: Harper & Row, 1989.

White, Suzanne. *The New Astrology.* New York: St. Martin's Press, 1986. Synthesis of Chinese and Western Astrological Systems.

Atlantis/Lemuria

> *ATLANTIS is believed to have been an advanced civilization which destroyed itself in a sudden nuclear-type explosion and disappeared beneath the Atlantic Ocean approximately 11,000 years ago.*

> *The continent of LEMURIA is said to have existed previous to Atlantis and sank into the Pacific Ocean during a shift of the Earth's axis.*

The name Atlantis calls to a soul memory as deep as the Atlantic Ocean itself. Plato first put the mystery of Atlantis to paper 2,500 years ago in his *Critias* and *Timaseus* dialogues. He described Atlantis as larger than Libya and Asia put together and the inhabitants of this eighth continent as civilized and evolved. According to Plato, complex canal systems, busy harbors, mighty fleets, and great cities with golden-roofed palaces decorated Atlantis. The Atlantean era was one of government and commerce, invention and advanced technology. Plato also wrote of the sudden end of this ancient metropolis through war — in "a terrible day and night" Atlantis sank under the ocean that bears its name.

Is Atlantis myth or memory? The case for its existence is continually mounting through modern day findings in geology, seismology, anthropology, linguistics, and oceanography. Even the most skeptical researchers are shifting uneasily under the ever growing weight of new evidence: Massive unexplained ruins left by unknown races *before* recorded history stand forgotten on both sides of the Atlantic Ocean; walls, roads and giant stone circles lie drowned in Bimini and in the Bermuda Triangle. The technique of carbon dating has proven that artifacts and mechanical devices were created thousands of years before our accepted timetable of history. Variations of the sounds A-T-L-N haunt the language of tribes and nations on both sides of the Atlantic Ocean. Through variations of the Noah's Ark story, the memory of an advanced civilization and its final destruction has been kept alive by ancient people of Europe, North Africa, and pre-Columbian tribes of the Americas.

If Atlantis really did exist, why did it perish? The channeled writings of Edgar Cayce, Ruth Montgomery, and many others advocate that the technology of the Atlantean people exceeded their level of consciousness. Greed, corruption, misuse of power, and disrespect for nature caused its final fall. Cayce and Montgomery both speak of a "Great Crystal" which was the source of energy for Atlantis and also its ultimate demise. They propose that this powerful crystal now lies under the Sargasso Sea and is the cause of the strange disappearances and electromagnetic interferences experienced in the Bermuda Triangle.

Cayce described the workings of the crystals of Atlantis and their highly powered "disciplined light" many years before the theory of laser technology had been expressed. He predicted that evidence for the lost continent of Atlantis would be discovered in Bimini (off the Florida coast) and more gold would be found there than was in circulation during 1935!

The name Lemuria was initiated in 1887 by Ernst Heinrich Haekel, a German biologist. Haekel studied the distribution of cute little squirrel-type critters called "lemurs" which inhabit various continents bordering on the Pacific Ocean, including the Comorro Islands, Africa, India, the Malay Peninsula, and Madagascar. Along with other researchers and their evidence, he theorized that an Indo-African land-bridge must once have existed in the Pacific in order for these animals to migrate. He named this land-bridge or continent, Lemuria.

Many researchers today believe that Lemuria, also referred to as Mu, flourished in the Pacific Ocean until it sank due to natural shifts in the Earth's surface. Ruth Montgomery has hailed Lemuria as the land of a gentle and spiritual people, whereas Atlantis "drew souls of a more scientific and technological inclination." She contends that Easter Island and parts of Hawaii are fragments of Lemuria and the islands' high vibrational energy (see VIBRATIONAL ENERGY/TONAL RESONANCE) is very healing even today.

In his book, *Lost Cities of Ancient Lemuria and the Pacific,* David Hatcher Childress reports that in nearly every religion in the world great civilizations, including Atlantis and Lemuria, existed in the past and were either destroyed through "internal conflict or as a result of some cataclysmic event." He continues:

Such traditions —legends —myths can be found in the Bible, the Ramayana, Chinese mythology, Hopi Indian legends, Mayan texts, African Tribal legends, Welsh and Scandinavian lore, Greek writings, Egyptian history, and Tibetan manuscripts (to name a few).

According to the famous astronomer, Carl Sagan, a book entitled, The True History of Mankind Over the Last 100,000 Years, once existed and was housed in the great library in Alexandria, Egypt. Unfortunately, this book, along with thousands of others, was burned by fanatical Christians in the third century A.D....

What a fascinating book that would have been to read! Perhaps our almost obsessive infatuation with these mythic lands of Atlantis and Lemuria is due to our civilization, seemingly, once again riding a roller coaster toward ruin. Much of today's channeled material maintains that thousands of souls who have chosen to incarnate at this time also lived during the destruction of Atlantis and are here trying to avert another such disaster.

Recommended Reading

Berlitz, Charles. *Atlantis: The Eighth Continent.* New York: Fawcett, 1984. Investigation into the question of Atlantis.

Cayce, Edgar. *Edgar Cayce on Atlantis.* New York: Warner Books, 1968. Accounts of past lives on the Lost Continent.

Childress, David Hatcher. *Lost Cities of Ancient Lemuria & the Pacific.* Stello, IL: Adventures Unlimited Press, 1988. Highly researched and well written.

Churchward, James. *The Children of Mu.* Sante Fe, NM: BE Books, reprintings 1987.

Churchward, James. *The Lost Continent of Mu.* Sante Fe, NM: BE Books, reprintings 1987.

Churchward, James. *The Sacred Symbols of Mu.* Sante Fe, NM: BE Books, reprinting 1987.

Montgomery, Ruth. *A World Before.* New York: Fawcett, 1985.

Muck, Otto. *The Secret of Atlantis.* New York: Simon & Schuster, Inc., 1976. A scientist's research and speculations about Atlantis.

Steiner, Rudolf. *Cosmic Memory.* Harper & Row, 1981. Includes a reconstruction of the achievements and fate of Atlantis and Lemuria.

Chants/Mantra/Om

> *CHANTS and MANTRAS are words or phrases spoken or sung repeatedly during meditation.*

> *OM is a sound used as a chant/mantra which denotes the creative force of the Universe.*

Chants and Mantras are used significantly in Tibetan Buddhism to help bring one to a higher state of consciousness. The literal meanings, or content, are not as important as the actual sound vibration emitted during the use of a Chant or Mantra. They are intended to be affirmations of faith and truth.

In Tibetan Buddhism, esoteric (see ESOTERIC) rituals such as Chanting create an altered state of consciousness. In *Open Secrets,* Walt Anderson relates that Buddhism teaches that it is futile to expect anything — your body, your state of consciousness, a relationship, even the world — to be the same from one moment to the next. The concept of impermanence, or continual change, is a firm underpinning of Buddhist teaching.

Om is a Chant used with an extended "m" — Ommmmmm — invoking the attention of the "creative force of being." "Om mani padme hum" used as a Chant or Mantra translates to "bow to the jewel within the lotus." The jewel being enlightenment within the human mind (lotus). The use of Om during a Mantra is to evoke or hail the infinite source of the cosmos. Again, the content is not as important during these meditations as the sound or tonal vibration qualities which can produce altered states of consciousness.

Recommended Reading

Anderson, Walt. *Open Secrets.* New York: The Viking Press, 1979. Guide to Tibetan Buddhism and insights to the use of Chanting and Mantras.

Batchelor, Stephen. *The Jewel in the Lotus.* London: Wisdom Publishing, 1987. A guide to Buddhist traditions.

Sherab Gyaltsen Amipa, Lama. *The Opening of the Lotus.* London: Wisdom Publishing, 1987.

Sivananda Radha, Swami. *Mantras: Words of Power.* Porthill, ID: Timeless Books, 1980.

Devas/Elementals

Devas/Elementals

DEVAS and ELEMENTALS are nature energies.
They are part of the plant or Earth kingdom.

The ancients accepted and cooperated with spirits of the plant kingdom. The archaic Hopi, Tibetan, and Celtic cultures knew how to listen to the elements of the Earth. They tended the soil with respect for its living energy and listened for advice from nature spirits on how best to cultivate their crops. Medieval philosophers believed an Elemental was a vortex of intelligent energy in constant motion. This universal energy took on the form of a "light body," or a glowing "etheric body" of the archetypal pattern for each plant, such as a Fairy, Gnome, or Elf.

Many believe that we, in our super-technological world, have lost our ability to hear the Devas. Devas are the caretakers of the Nature World, responsible for the emergence and manifestation of each unique pattern of plant into physical form. Presently, a few people still profess they can see and hear the Devas, Tree Spirits, and Elementals of the Nature World. One such group of individuals formed the Findhorn Community (see CENTERS OF LIGHT/NEW AGE COM-MUNITIES) in Glasgow, Scotland. In 1962, Peter and Eileen Caddy, their three sons, and their close friend Dorothy Maclean parked their trailer on a narrow sandy peninsula. The soil was constantly swept by wind and was composed of sand, gravel, stones, and couch grass. However, they began a pioneering experiment to work *with* nature, seeking to cooperate with the inner spirit of each plant rather than manipulating its outer form.

They listened for guidance from the Devas on how to organically protect, plant, nurture, energize, and fertilize their seedlings. Within two years their small garden was filled with such vitality that it attracted world-wide attention. Through the channeled energy and advice of the Devas and Elementals, they had produced fruit and vegetables far beyond their natural pattern of growth, i.e., one red cabbage weighed in at 38 pounds, another at 42, and a white sprouting broccoli grew to such proportions that it was nearly too heavy to lift!

The Findhorn Community has been extensively studied and written about by scientists, parapsychologists, and horticulturists. The sensitivity of its founders to these paraphysical beings and energies of nature has transformed Findhorn from a barren sandy piece of beach into a veritable garden of Eden blooming with flowers and flourishing with over 128 varieties of vegetables, fruits, and herbs.

Recommended Reading

The Findhorn Community. *The Findhorn Garden.* New York: Harper & Row, 1975. A joy to peruse.

Hawken, Paul. *The Magic of Findhorn.* New York: Harper & Row, 1976.

Esoteric

ESOTERIC means secret knowledge that is known by a select few.

Esoteric doctrines were only intended for an inner circle of initiates. Special rituals, healing with herbs, Esoteric knowledge of astrology and numerology were among the confidential wisdoms handed down to others through secret societies. Many esoteric schools were forced to go "underground" with their teachings during certain restrictive periods of history. Private benevolent societies, such as the Freemasons and the Rosicrucians were devoted to the pursuit of a moral philosophy of life. Both of these international fraternal orders were not permitted in some strictly Roman Catholic countries. Their binding principles and religious nature were seen as usurping the prerogatives of the church.

The Masonic concept was one of religious tolerance, in that choice of religion was the concern solely of the individual. It also taught the basic equality of all people. The Rosicrucians take their name from the symbol of the rose and the cross and hold that their Esoteric wisdom began in the antiquity of Egypt. These doctrines combine elements of Gnosticism, Jewish Cabalism, Egyptian Hermetism and other metaphysical (see METAPHYSICS) ideals.

Recommended Reading

Blavatsky, Helen P. *The Secret Doctrine.* Wheaton, IL: The Theosophical Publishing House, reprinting 1980. Three volumes of heavy, but insightful, reading.

Incognito, Magnus. *Secret Doctrine of the Rosicrucians.* IL: Yoga Publishing Society, no date.

Rosicrucian Digest. Rosicrucian Order. AMORC, Rosicrucian Park, San Jose, CA 95191. Bimonthly magazine publication.

Satprem. *Mother of the Divine Materialism.* New York: Foundation for Evolutionary Research, 1979.

Urantia Foundation. *The Urantia Book.* Chicago, IL: Urantia Foundation, 1955.

Guru/Murshid/Shaman

> *A GURU, MURSHID, or SHAMAN is one who has mastered the spiritual levels within their own being and is a teacher of a specific spiritual system or tradition.*

In the Hindu religion a personal spiritual guide is called a Guru. Translated from Sanskrit, Guru means "that which dispels darkness." A Murshid, or Murshida if female, is regarded as a master teacher of the Sufi religion. In the Shamanic tradition, a Shaman is a counselor or wise one who has travailed some personal illness or challenge and in having been healed has become a healer of others. Throughout history these awakened teachers have assumed the role of intermediary between their peers and the spirit world.

Meher Baba describes an authentic Guru as one who has realized on all levels "to penetrate into the essence of all being and significance and to release the fragrance of that inner attainment for the guidance and benefit of others — by expressing, in the world of forms, truth, love, purity and beauty — is the sole game which has intrinsic and absolute worth."

The student studying under the guidance of a Guru is called a disciple. This relationship can be a sensitive and meaningful union. However, there is always a danger in giving away one's personal power (see PERSONAL POWER) to another. In many cases the teacher/disciple relationship has been abused. If in following your own "Guruwithin" you are compelled to seek guidance from a reputable spiritual teacher, it is wise to enter such a relationship with eyes wide open — for even when following the advice of a Guru, you are accountable and personally responsible for *your* life.

Recommended Reading

Andrews, Lynn. *Jaguar Woman.* New York. Harper & Row, 1986. A Shamanic Initiation.

Andrews, Lynn. *Medicine Woman.* New York: Harper & Row, 1983.

Doore, Gary, editor. *Shaman's Path.* Boston, MA: Shambhala, 1988.

Duce, Ivy O., Murshida and Dr. James Mackie. *Gurus and Psychotherapists: Spiritual Versus Psychological Learning.* California: Searchlight Publications, 1981. A no-nonsense framework of questions and answers about Gurus and spiritual teachers.

Knight, Carol Bell. *Passing the Torch.* Walpole, NH: Stillpoint Publishing, 1985. Refinement of spiritual consciousness through the ever-present cycle of the student-teacher relationship.

Yogananda, Paramahansa. *Autobiography of a Yogi.* Los Angeles: Self-Realization Fellowship, 1974. A rare personal account.

Yungblut, John R. *The Gentle Art of Spiritual Guidance.* New York: Amity House, Inc., 1990. Practical handbook for those who guide others or seek to be guided along the spiritual path.

Hypnosis/Hypnotherapy

HYPNOSIS is a tool to reach the subconscious mind.
HYPNOTHERAPY is a form of therapy which utilizes
the techniques of hypnosis as well as other counseling
methods.

Hypnosis is an altered state of consciousness (see ALTERED STATES OF CONSCIOUSNESS) shown to be between the awakening "beta" state of consciousness and the sleeping "delta" state.

To induce a state of Hypnosis one can learn the techniques themselves or go to a therapist to be guided into this relaxing trance. Once in this state of relaxation it becomes very easy to direct or stimulate the subconscious mind. With the tools and techniques from Self-Hypnosis, one can program the subconscious in a variety of positive ways. Self-Hypnosis and guided Hypnosis can be used to break a habit, alleviate fears and phobias, reduce stress, relieve pain, and enhance memory.

Hypnotherapy is a form of therapy combining the trance induction of Hypnosis with individualized techniques of counseling secured by each Hypnotherapist uniquely. Therefore, Hypnotherapy cannot be confined within a detailed description. Every Hypnotherapist has specialized tools, techniques, and background specifically directed to the counseling field. Hypnotherapy encompasses a holistic approach to health and healing, looking at the total person's health and well-being.

Within the sessions of Hypnotherapy one may discover hidden memories, latent creativity, new insights, feelings of competence, release fears, or touch a deep emotion. Whatever the situation or process, Hypnotherapy is presented as "...a dramatically rapid intervention system which strengthens and reshapes the client's feelings of competence and capability," says Gil Boyne, the Executive Director of the American Council of Hypnotist Examiners.

In Hypnotherapy one can come to the realization that we are responsible for our own realities and can choose to change or re-create (see RE-CREATION) our perceptions and beliefs to create a reality by choice, not mere acceptance of what we believe we must accept. This "consciousness of self" or awakening of awareness is one of the highest rewards of Hypnotherapy.

Another reward derived from the use of Hypnosis and Hypnotherapy is that of discovering an avenue for controlling stress and anxiety. In today's fast-paced world many of us have not allowed ourselves the time and techniques to shift our attention to being alone with ourselves and quieting the external and internal strains of our lives. Stress is an instinctual reaction to any anxiety-producing situation. Some stress is healthy — what is important to our health is how we deal with the stresses which confront us daily. Hypnosis and Hypnotherapy are alternatives which help the pieces fit to ensure a state of wholeness.

Recommended Reading

Hadley, Josie, and Carol Staudacher. *Hypnosis for Change.* New York: Ballantine Books, 1987. A thorough manual with practical techniques.

Kelly, Sean, and Reid. *Hypnosis: Understanding How It Can Work For You.* Reading, MA: Addison-Wesley Publishing Co., 1985. Searches into the history of theory, inductions, and other medical uses of Hypnosis/Hypnotherapy.

Morris, Freda. *Hypnosis with Friends and Lovers.* New York: Harper & Row, 1979. Creative uses for Hypnosis.

Tebbetts, Charles. *Self-Hypnosis: The Creative Use of Your Mind for Successful Living.* Los Angeles: Westwood Publishing Co., 1985. Great starter book for the beginner.

CH'IEN
乾
HEAVEN

TUI
兌
LAKE

SUN
巽
WIND

LI
離
FIRE

K'AN
坎
WATER

SUMMER
S

SPRING
E

FALL
W

WINTER
N

THUNDER
CHEN
震

KEN
艮
MOUNTAIN

EARTH
K'UN
坤

I Ching

I Ching

> *The I CHING (pronounced "e" ching) is a Chinese philosophically-based oracle which guides the unconscious to function in the present moment.*

The *I Ching* is an oracle of the wisdom of change. It was developed over three thousand years ago in China and is a source of reference in both Confucianism and Taoism. The philosophy of the *I Ching* explores the unconscious mind of the reader and opens a channel to the movement of the present. It aids the person seeking self-knowledge through thoughtful reflection. These aspects, combined with synchronicity (see SYNCHRONICITY), give rise to insight and understanding. The synchronistic view of the Chinese deals with the "coincidence of events" — not mere causality. The meaningful string of events or situations become then, the reality of constant change — not mere cause and effect philosophy. Therefore, the *I Ching* may not be for the scientifically-minded, but will prove enticing for a viewer of the wisdom of change.

The *I Ching* acts like a triggering device for the unconscious. It unveils the clouds of fear, doubt, resignation, and so on; thus, one can literally hear the truth surrounding a situation. As renowned author and psychotherapist, Carl Jung, put it, the *I Ching* answers "...the questioner's psychological blind spot." The answers become the awaited channel of understanding that light the way to truth.

To interpret the *I Ching*, one needs only a workbook of meanings and three coins. The workbook has the interpretations of how the coins are thrown. The coins are thrown six times creating a hexagram or reading. There are sixty-four possible combinations of hexagrams with the same number of interpretations. Using the *I Ching* is a simple sequence of procedures and can be learned quickly. The *I Ching* method of looking within for answers is not for everyone. As Jung further explains:

> *The I Ching does not offer itself with proofs and results; it does not vaunt itself, nor is it easy to approach. Like a part of nature, it waits until it is discovered. It offers neither facts nor power, but for lovers of self-knowledge, of wisdom — if there be such — it seems to be the right book. To one person its spirit appears*

as clear as day; to another, shadowy as twilight; to a third, dark as night. He who is not pleased by it does not have to use it, and he who is against it is not obliged to find it true. Let it go forth into the world for the benefit of those who can discern its meaning.

Recommended Reading

Huang, Kerson. *I Ching: The Oracle.* New York: Workman Publishers, 1987.

Reifler, Sa. *I Ching.* New York: Bantam Books, 1986. A new interpretation for modern times.

Stein, Diane. *The Kwan Yin Book of Changes.* St. Paul, MN: Llewellyn Publications, 1985.

Wilhelm, Richard, translator. *The I Ching - or Book of Changes.* Princeton, NJ: Princeton University Press, 1985. A thorough edition of the reading and interpretations of the I Ching.

Wing, R.L. *The Illustrated I Ching.* New York: Dolphin Books/Doubleday & Co., Inc., 1982. A beginner's guide and workbook for the I Ching.

Karma

KARMA, translated from Sanskrit, simply means action and is the universal principle of "cause and effect." It is not a law of punishment or retribution but one of balance and opportunity for development.

Karmic law forms the basis for much of the world's religions. It is the most famous of all spiritual principles and was also expressed biblically — "like begets like," and "you reap what you sow." In modern terminology we could consider Karma a "feed-back" system. Throughout life we sow seeds of kindness, anger, love, jealousy, strength, and victimhood. What we choose to plant we shall one day harvest.

Author and psychologist William James expressed that we are spinning our own fates, good or evil, and every stroke of virtue or vice leaves its scar. Every person, thing, and situation we encounter is the result of our previous thoughts, actions, and reactions. Over time, reincarnation (see REINCARNATION) and Karma in their evolutionary wisdom enable us to widen our understanding of ourselves and our universe through experience. We fill the gaps of ignorance from lifetime to lifetime as Karma stirs us toward self-transformation.

Reincarnation and Karma are but two sides of a single coin. Personal growth in each life influences the lineup of dynamics that will follow in subsequent life-spans. When an area of development remains unresolved at the conclusion of one's life, physical circumstances in other incarnations will set up the lesson anew. We are creating "good Karma" when we handle this adversity creatively. The challenge is to shift perception and realize that Karma is what we really *want* — what we have chosen to work on in our current life to bring us into healing and wholeness.

We choose our reality and with that knowledge is the acceptance that all karmic-happenstance is shared. Ultimately, there are three layers of karmic influence, they are: individual, personal Karma; national Karma; and ethnic or racial Karma. If a man murders another man, karmic questions arise: Who made the gun? Who sold it? How did movies, society, and family influence his tragic cry for help?

We are born through parents with whom we share a karmic affinity. We are spun in a karmic web with "fellow adventurers" whom we call mother, father, sister, brother, or "significant others." Our relationships are neither punishment nor reward, but a joint passage into greater equilibrium. Forgiveness (see FORGIVENESS) and understanding can reverse the karmic wheel of action. Karma sets up the framework but the outcome is never assured or predestined. From the channeled writing of Agartha, we learn:

When one begins to play within the natural laws of manifestation, karmic debt is released. Once attunement and awareness have been gained, the confinements of karma have been transcended. One exists within karmic debt only so long as one is willing to exist within karmic debt....

Disease, imbalance or any lack of wholeness, even though it springs to life through karma, cannot stand in the aura of love without being transmuted.

Recommended Reading

Cayce, Edgar. Marian Woodward, editor. *Edgar Cayce's Story of Karma.* New York: Berkeley Books, 1972. Cayce's wisdom shines once again.

Elwell, Lynn. *Reincarnation: Claiming Your Past, Creating Your Future.* New York: Sparrow, Harper & Row, 1988.

Hanson, Virginia, and Rosemarie Stewart. *Karma: Universal Law of Harmony.* Wheaton, IL: The Theosophical Publishing House, 1980. A common sense look at Karma.

Iyer, Raghavan, editor. *Karma.* Santa Barbara, CA: Concord Grove Press, 1984. A collection of essays dealing with cosmic harmony and ethical causation.

Kundalini

KUNDALINI is the psychic energy, or force, generating a physiological experience which in turn arouses the spiritual or superconscious nature.

In the Indian tradition there are chakra centers which radiate the life-force within the body. At the base of the spine is the root chakra, this is the first energy wheel entwined by the archetypal serpent goddess. This healing force called Kundalini is the activating principle which connects all the chakra centers. When this Kundalini is activated it is generally a unique and powerful experience which can result in a profound change in consciousness. This psychic event may last from hours to months in duration. The activation of Kundalini energy can lead to many different spiritual and/or psychic behaviors or experiences. Extra-clear or potent dreams can be one of the results of Kundalini energy rising.

When one studies the medical emblem, the Caduceus, the Kundalini life-force is found within the symbol of the serpents wrapping themselves around the staff-of-life. This Kundalini serpent energy lies coiled at the base of the spine in the root chakra. When it becomes activated by a psychic event or spiritual awakening this snake also awakens and begins to rise up the spine to open each chakra energy center. This gradual ascent is the awakening of consciousness and personal responsibility. Carl Jung referred to the Kundalini energy as the *anima* (see YIN/YANG, ANIMA/ANIMUS) or the spirit of adventure. Kundalini may be experienced as the divine discontent which pulls one out of the mundane to embark on the inward journey of self-realization.

Recommended Reading

Judith, Anodea. *Wheels of Life.* St. Paul, MN: Llewellyn Publications, 1987. Details the Kundalini energy.

Krishna, Gopi. *Kundalini: Evolutionary Energy in Man.* Boston: Shambhala, 1970. Personal account of a Kundalini experience.

Mookerjee, Ajit. *Kundalini: The Arousal of the Inner Energy.* Rochester,VT: Destiny Books, 1986 (Inner Traditions Intntl., Ltd.).

Sannella, Lee. *Kundalini: Psychosis or Transcendence?* Lower Lake, CA: Integral Publishing, 1987. Viewing case histories.

Sivananda Radha, Swami. *Kundalini Yoga for the West.* Porthill, ID: Timeless Books, 1981.

Meditation

Practiced for centuries in all cultures, MEDITATION is a process of controlling thought patterns that seek to join infinite levels of consciousness to achieve inner peace and serenity.

Although some yogis have been known to enter a deep meditative state for hours or days at a time, Meditation need not be time consuming. A few minutes a day is all that is needed to establish a connection between the physical self and the spiritual nature.

Meditation can be practiced in many different forms through many different schools and by many different means: yogic; transcendental; T'ai Chi; by playing a musical instrument; writing; painting; singing; by reciting a mantra (see CHANTS/MANTRA/OM) or poetry; through jogging or breathing exercises. Meditation can be a soothing and successful method for releasing the day's tension and for creating time that is free of anxiety. It is a process that rejuvenates the vital energies, allowing for clearer vision and a more positive mental capacity.

Meditation can be most easily accomplished in a quiet, comfortable place where you feel confident you will not be disturbed. Sitting or lying in a comfortable position, close your eyes. Contemplate or reflect upon any thought, idea, object or picture, a piece of music — anything that can totally absorb your attention. Many people concentrate on the sixth chakra, the area of the forehead just above the bridge of the nose associated with an energy center or revitalizing point called the "third eye" (see THIRD EYE).

When meditating, your entire consciousness should be focused on one thought. This act of concentration is transportation to a higher level of consciousness. Meditation is the emptying of self of all that hinders. By letting go of our hindrances, we free ourselves to enjoy the experience of simply *being.* Whatever technique is used to meditate, most people find that regular practice provides a long-lasting sense of peace and well-being.

Recommended Readings

Goleman, Daniel. *The Meditative Mind.* Los Angeles: J.P. Tarcher, Inc., 1988. All forms of Meditative practices.

LeShan, Lawrence. *How to Meditate: A Guide to Self-Discovery.* New York: Bantam Books, 1986.

Pipkin, Wayne. *Christian Meditation: Its Art and Practice.* New York: Hawthorn Books, Inc., 1977.

Ram Dass. *Journey of Awakening: A Meditator's Guidebook.* New York: Bantam Books, 1978.

Schwarz, Jack. *The Path of Action.* New York: E.P. Dutton, 1977. Spiritually directed material.

White, John, editor. *What Is Meditation?* New York: Doubleday/Anchor Press, 1974. Anthology exploring meditation.

Mystic/Mysticism

A MYSTIC is a person devoted to mysticism.

MYSTICISM is a way of life, within a spiritual context, which centers on the transformation of an individual and ultimately touches group consciousness.

To the Mystic, only the present is important. This present creates the future in an ever unfolding transformation. Our dreams, visions, and thoughts keep our reality alive. As Mystic Sri Aurobindo said so poetically:

The universe is an endless masquerade:
For nothing here is utterly what it seems,
It is a dream-fact vision of a truth
Which but for the dream would not be wholly true.

The Mystic's way is one of constantly re-evaluating every experience, every relationship, to create a more positive consciousness. The word mystical is derived from the Greek word, *mystos*, which means "keeping silence." The practice of Mysticism is an "internal process" of transforming reality.

Mysticism is not a religion (see SPIRITUAL/RELIGIOUS), not an occult practice, and not just a philosophy. Mystics do not define or label, they do not allow mental boundaries, limit God by definition, or limit their thoughts on life. Mysticism says, "Not we — but One," therefore reiterating the total unity or oneness of all.

The evolutionary path of Mysticism often includes the concepts of karma and reincarnation. The nature of karma is cause and effect. Our actions (cause) are seeds — reactions (effect) are fruit. Eventually, one must recognize how karma is a part of the Oneness of life. The accumulation of experience over many lifetimes serves to evolve, or transform, an individual's spiritual progress. This individual evolvement is then reflected in group consciousness, or the human evolution. Mystic Meher Baba summed it up perfectly when he said, "...because, in the end, there is but one Man. One single evolution. We all arrive at the goal together, or no one arrives."

Recommended Reading

Bharati, Agehananda. *The Light at the Center.* Santa Barbara, CA: Ross-Erikson Publishing, Inc., 1976. Studies in modern Mysticism.

Happold, F.C. *Mysticism: A Study and an Anthology.* New York: Penguin Books, 1985. A thorough introduction.

LeShan, Lawrence. *The Medium, the Mystic, and the Physicist.* New York: Ballantine Books, 1982.

Meher Baba. *The Everything and the Nothing.* Australia: Meher House Publications, 1976. A book of teachings.

Satprem. *Sri Aurobindo or the Adventure of Consciousness.* New York: Institute for Evolutionary Research, 1984.

Stage, W.T. *Mysticism & Philosophy.* Los Angeles: J.P. Tarcher, Inc., 1960. In-deptn look at the Mystic.

Numerology

> *NUMEROLOGY is an ancient study of number systems. This esoteric art is based on the theory that numbers represent energy patterns and vibrations which are said to affect destiny.*

The power of certain numbers is mentioned in many religious books including *The Bible* and the *Upanishads,* i.e., the seven days of creation, the seven Seals, the seven Amsha-Spands of Persia, the seven Sephiroth of the *Cabbalah,* the seven Archangels of Revelations, the seven spirits of the Egyptian religion, the seven Devas of Hinduism, and we could go on and on until we all meet in seventh heaven!

Winston Churchill swore by the number one, Swoboda by twenty-three, Sigmund Freud believed in periods of twenty-seven, and Goethe was obsessed with the number three. Since the earliest times numbers have possessed special significance. Through endless repetition in human experience number-symbols have been engraved in the collective unconscious (see COLLECTIVE UNCONSCIOUS). These archetypes (see ARCHETYPAL SYMBOLS) have specific meaning and metaphysical value.

Like astrology and palmistry, Numerology is a blueprint which reveals clues about one's unique vibratory karmic pattern. One's Numerology should dove-tail quite predictably with the lines in one's palm and the stars in one's astrological configuration. It is proposed that through Numerology one can discover his or her hidden talents and what obstacles may hinder success. Each number from one to nine has an inner dynamic-energy and corresponds to a letter in the alphabet.

Key of Numbers and Their Corresponding Letters

1	2	3	4	5	6	7	8	9	Master Numbers
A	B	C	D	E	F	G	H	I	11
J	K	L	M	N	O	P	Q	R	22
S	T	U	V	W	X	Y	Z	&	33

Your total name tells you the direction to take to fulfill your purpose in life. A suffix such as "Senior" or "Junior" is omitted in calculations, just as the prefix of "Doctor," "Mr." and "Mrs." are not actually part of one's name vibration.

The first step to finding your life purpose is to write your *full* name recorded at birth and place the numerical value directly under each appropriate letter. Then reduce individual names to a single digit (do not reduce Master Numbers of 11 and 22). Add the subtotals to find the final total of the entire name. (A brief summary of the general meaning of numbers is listed below and on the following page). Below is an example:

```
MARTIN   LUTHER   KING
419295   332859   2957
reduced =   30      30      23
reduced =    3       3       5    = 11
```

Three plus three plus five equals a life purpose number of eleven, which is a *master* number. This signifies that King was an idealist, a visionary and an inspiration to others. He was destined for the platform, giving speeches or sermons. If he were to live up to his soul's purpose or calling he would serve in a crusade for the betterment of humanity — and this he most certainly did!

The above example represents only one of the simplest forms in which the science of Numerology can be explored. Adding vowels and consonants separately determines one's secret ambitions and the key to one's personality. The name also holds one's destiny or expression numbers and these added to one's birthday determines yet another aspect of a person's source of power or goals in life. Numerology also tells us about our stumbling blocks, potentialities, talents, and karmic patterns.

Summary of General Meaning and Characteristics of Numbers in a Name *

1 = ambition, invention, pioneer, leader, individualist
2 = diplomacy, service, rhythm, detailed, peacemaker
3 = self-expression, optimism, sociability, humorist
4 = builder, organization, honesty, practicality, loyal
5 = traveler, adventurer, versatility, progress, change

6 = teacher, domesticity, responsibility, musical talents
7 = thinker, philosopher, psychic, perfectionist, study

8 = analyst, executive ability, management, authority
9 = philanthropist, humanitarian, artistic, healer, spiritual
11 = idealist, religion, intuitive, inspiration, speaker,
    diplomat
22 = internationalist, practical master builder, powerful,
    ambassador, president
33 = avatar, spiritual master, universal leader of a
    movement

*Based on *Helping Yourself With Numbers,* by Helyn Hitchcock.

Recommended Reading

Adrienne, Carol. *The Numerology Kit.* New York: New American Library, 1988. All you need to know about Numerology.

Campbell, Florence. *Your Days are Numbered.* Marina del Rey, CA: DeVorss & Co., Inc., 1987.

Connolly, Eileen. *The Connolly Book of Numbers.* North Hollywood, CA: Newcastle Publishing Co., Inc., 1988. Unique approaches to numbers.

Cooper, D. Jason. *Numerology: The Power to Know Anybody.* Great Britain: The Aquarian Press, 1986.

Dodge, Ellin. *Numerology Has Your Number.* New York: Simon & Schuster, Inc., 1988. A positive approach.

Hitchcock, Helyn. *Helping Yourself with Numerology.* New York: Parker Publishing Co., Inc., 1972. Numerology made easy as one, two, three.

Palmistry/Hand Analysis

Palmistry/Hand Analysis

PALMISTRY/HAND ANALYSIS is an overall study of the hands including, the palms; finger and thumb shapes; texture and color of the skin; "lines of flexure;" the fingerprint patterns that cover the palm and fingertips; and the various markings, such as circles, squares, crosses, triangles, stars, and dots.

Palmistry was regarded as a serious study among the ancient Egyptians, Chinese, Hindus, and Jews. Throughout history we have sought to discover our fate by gazing into the unique pattern inscribed in our palms. Modern science has found that like the electromagnetic field, or aura (see AURA), one's palm print depends on sustained changes in signals from the brain. Mental and emotional conditions cause changes in the hands. Lines in the palms break down when impulses from the brain cease at death. Thus, Palmistry is considered by many to be a science based on psychology or one's psyche. We actually possess very explicit information right at our fingertips.

The creases, or flexure lines of the hands, alter with inward or outward experience or change. In a thirty-day period dramatic alterations occurred in the flexure lines of a police officer who was forced (in self-defense) to shoot a person to death. This incident affected him tremendously. He questioned himself and his beliefs while undergoing deep transformative changes. This personal growth in turn altered his psyche or personality and his change in consciousness was mirrored in the "life blueprint" of his palm.

In *Supernatural*, biologist Lyall Watson reports another fascinating case of metamorphosis in palm patterns:

> *There is one dramatic record of a house painter who fell from a great height and suffered such severe concussion that he remained unconscious for two weeks and had to be intravenously fed. After a week in this condition, all the creases in his hands vanished as though they had been wiped-off with a sponge —and then, as he regained consciousness, the lines gradually reappeared. Unlike the lines of flexure, dermatoglyphics —which translates to "skin carvings" —do not change. Fingerprints and skin patterns begin to form prena-*

tally around thirteen weeks and these unique markings are unalterable from the moment of birth.

Richard Unger is one of the world's leading authorities on Hand Analysis and editor of the "Hand Analysis Journal." He has noted that these unalterable ripples or ridges (known as pattern "minutiae") are also found in masses of sand which have been swept by moving air or water. These patterns have also been observed in some cloud formations and in certain reducing chemical suspensions. In other words, Unger states, "Wave vibrations passing over a denser medium are capable of leaving an imprint and we can learn the nature of the vibration by a study of the impression left behind." He goes on to theorize:

If our physical bodies are but one expression of a higher vibrationary energy (i.e., spirit) it seems reasonable that we may study this energy by the impressions left on our own skins during our formation process.

Your hand mirrors your avoidance behaviors, motivation, hidden talents, relationship patterns, and gives an accurate picture of your personal evolutionary plan.

A scientific base for Hand Analysis is fast becoming apparent. The ridge and furrow patterns of the hands have become the subject of serious study in genetics, medicine, anthropology, biology, and psychology. Scientists, doctors, and psychologists have established links between particular skin patterns and chromosomal abnormalities, such as: approximately thirty different congenital disorders; certain pathological conditions; thyroid deficiency; spinal deformation; liver and kidney malfunctions; infectious diseases; tuberculosis; and even cancer. It is suggested that many of these diseases and/or mental states may be traceable through dermatoglyphics *before* their appearance in the body or psyche. It seems Palmists are not the only people interested in reading hands. Don't be too surprised if during your next physical exam your doctor asks you to stick out your hand instead of your tongue!

Recommended Reading

Altman, Nathaniel. *Sexual Palmistry.* Great Britain: The Aquarian Press, 1986. Fascinating and Fun.

Anderson, Mary. *Palmistry.* Great Britain: The Aquarian Press, 1980. "How to read the visible part of your brain."

Asano, Hachiro. *Hands: The Complete Book of Palmistry.* Tokyo: Japan Publications, 1985.

Brandon-Jones, David. *Practical Palmistry.* Reno, NV: CRCS Publications, 1986. Up-to-date and informative.

Cheiro. *Cheiro's Palmistry for All.* New York: Prentice-Hall, Inc., 1964.

Fenton, Sasha and Malcom Wright. *The Living Hand.* Great Britain: The Aquarian Press, 1986. Interesting case histories to illustrate their findings.

Prayer

PRAYER or the act of praying is the communication with a Higher Source, Infinite Being, God/Goddess/All That Is.

Prayer is defined as a *petition*; a petition is a formal *request*. Praying to a Higher Being is a type of communication in which one can "ask for" help, forgiveness, healing, or give "thanks for" such occurrences. While praying is the communication *to,* meditation (see MEDITATION) becomes the communication *from* a Higher Source.

The act of praying can be a door to awakening the divinity within. For some of us, it takes practice to learn and/or remember to pray in thankfulness instead of petitioning. Praying becomes more natural as we consciously affirm its use and acknowledge its blessings.

Praying to the Infinite guiding force takes many shapes. The most common term evoked with the word prayer is *request*, a petition or asking for something, i.e., healing for self or others, material gains, success in love relationships, the birth of a baby, and so on. When we feel we have done all *we* can regarding a situation, we turn to prayer (sometimes as a last resort). Usually this becomes a desperate plea for help to a Higher Being in which we believe.

However, it is pertinent to remember to also give thanks in prayer while the fullness of success, happy relationship, or wholeness in health is present. As Kahlil Gibran wrote so many years ago, "For what is prayer but the expansion of yourself into the living ether?" *We* are that living ether — if you project darkness, fear, and doubt so shall you receive. Instead, pour delight and thankfulness into your prayers and reap their rewards.

Someone once said, "Worrying is praying backward." Remember the power of your mind and the manifestation principle of your thought. Praying can occur through direct conscious communication, or unconscious thought. Frank Laubach, author of *Prayer: The Mightiest Force in the World,* writes, "If you shout, your voice carries barely fifty yards. But when you think, your thoughts go around the world, as far and as fast as the radio...every thought we think is helping or harming other people." Learn to pray continually, in health, joy, and forgiveness, to spiral the much needed positive manifestation of Unity into our universe (see UNITY/ONENESS).

Another form of prayer is group praying. When "two or more are gathered in His name" is a familiar phrase reminding us of the power of group prayer. There are various groups within the world, such as Unity, Science of Mind, and The Association for Research and Enlightenment that specifically hold group prayer sessions at regular intervals every day. We can, as a group, learn to hold a prayer in our minds and hearts allowing thoughts of health, peace, and unity to unfold over the world. This type of praying is exactly what transpired during the August, 1987 Harmonic Convergence event.

Recommended Reading

Daily Word. Colleen Zuck, editor. Silent Unity's Magazine. MO: Unity School of Christianity. Prayers and affirmations written for each day of the year.

Gibran, Kahlil. *The Prophet.* New York: Alfred A. Knopf, original printing 1923. Inspirational prayer communication.

Karunananda, Swami, editor. *Lotus Prayer Book.* Buckingham, VA: Integral Yoga Publications, 1986. A collection of prayers from all the major faiths.

Puryear, Meredith Ann. *Healing Through Meditation & Prayer.* Virginia Beach, VA: A.R.E. Press, 1978. Insight based on the Edgar Cayce readings.

Vaughan, Francis, and Roger Walsh, editors. *Accept This Gift.* Selections from A Course in Miracles. Los Angeles: J.P. Tarcher Inc., 1983. Prayers in poetry.

Prophet/Avatar

> *A PROPHET or AVATAR is a spiritually enlightened being who has incarnated into physical form.*

Christ, Buddha, Krishna, Rama, Babaji are among the highly evolved souls who have chosen to bless our Earth with their physical presence. A divinely-inspired soul is beyond the wheel of karma and is no longer *required* to return to physical manifestation. However, throughout time great Prophets and Avatars have descended into flesh for a specific and spectacular purpose and have left their bodies as soon as their mission on Earth was accomplished.

These God-beings radiate a complex spherical pattern of energy. This high frequency vibration (see VIBRATIONAL ENERGY/ TONAL RESONANCE) is responsible for the halo or auric glow which artists have captured on canvas and all great holy scriptures have documented.

It is believed that there are seven vibratory levels or octaves which manifest in human consciousness. The average person radiates vibrations up to the fourth plane, the genius up to the fifth, the prophet up to the sixth, and the Avatar or God-being is able to consciously radiate all seven octaves. The fifth plane of consciousness is divine wisdom, the sixth plane is universal love without attachment or separation, and the seventh octave expresses divine unity with the Infinite All.

An Avatar does not possess an unconscious mind, he or she is perfected *consciousness* and thus has access to all past, present, and future knowledge. A fully-illumined Master can perform miracles (see MIRACLES). They can materialize form from energy and then hold this illusion together through the power of their will.

Recommended Reading

Adriel, Jean. *Avatar.* California: The Beguine Library, 1947. The story of Avatar Meher Baba.

Hesse, Hermann. *Siddhartha.* New York: New Directions Publishing Corporation, 1951. You won't want to put it down.

Yogananda, Paramahansa. *Autobiography of a Yogi.* Los Angeles: Self-Realization Fellowship, 1946. Rich personal experiences of spiritual adventure and contact with divine beings.

Epstein, Perle. *Kabbalah: The Way of the Jewish Mystic.* Boston: Shambhala Publications, 1988.

Ghanananda, Swami. *Women Saints of East and West.* Hollywood, CA: Vedanta Press, 1979.

Kersten, Holger. *Jesus lived in India.* Great Britain: Elemert Book, Ltd., 1988. Speculation and factual findings of the unknown life of Jesus before and after the crucifixion.

Lings, Martin. *Muhammad: His Life Based on the Earliest Sources.* Rochester, VT: Inner Traditions International, LTD., 1987. Based on Arabic sources of the eighth and nineth centuries.

Pyramid Power/Pyramidology

PYRAMID POWER refers to the energy harnessed within the structure of a pyramid.

PYRAMIDOLOGY is the term used to describe the study of pyramids.

For centuries humankind has been captivated by the great Pyramids built on our planet thousands of years ago. What is so compelling about the shape of a Pyramid? Are there secret powers held within them? What goes on inside a Pyramid?

Questions like the ones above have been pondered for centuries by people captivated by the "spell" of the great Pyramids of the world. If you have seen pictures of any of these wonders, you are aware of the immense size and weight of the stones placed perfectly to form exact Pyramid shapes. The great Cheops Pyramid found near Cairo in Egypt contains over two-and-one-half million blocks of stone. Each of these stones fit together perfectly leaving only a trace of a line distinguishing one block from the other. This fact becomes unbelievable when we realize that each of these blocks of stone weighs as much as 70 tons and the Pyramid covers approximately thirteen acres of land. How these giant structures were built is still being questioned today.

Learning about the power of the Pyramid can be an exciting adventure. Many of the experiments can be completed in your own home with a few tools and materials. To give you an example of the many areas where one can gain insight into pyramidology and the powerful energy contained in each pyramid, check this list of tests which have uncovered the secrets of the Pyramid.

When placed within a Pyramid structure it is said that:

- *Food does not decay.*
- *Razor blades remain sharp.*
- *Water and air become and stay purified.*
- *Plants grow from two to three times faster.*
- *Animals live longer than normal.*
- *One's meditation is enhanced.*
- *One's need for sleep is decreased.*

These and other miraculous findings have been discovered and experimented with by the scientific community.

You can construct your own Pyramid with materials such as cardboard, wood, plastics, glass, canvas, or anything nonmetallic. The main consideration in constructing a Pyramid is the key angle, or slope of the sides of the Pyramid to the floor. Placing plants, foods, or anything you wish to give energy, or power, into your Pyramid can produce noticeable effects.

The literal meaning of the word pyramid is "fire in the middle." This definition alludes to the fact that fire means transformation (see TRANSFORMATION/TRANSCENDENCE). Fire can also be interpreted as light. This light energy, or power, found within a Pyramid can be harnessed and used for constructive purposes. In fact, the Department of Agriculture has experimented with Pyramids by placing 30-inch-base Pyramids in cow pastures with a resultant seventy percent reduction in flies and other insects. Also, in an attempt to reduce pollution and water contamination, water treated by Pyramid energy for two weeks produced fewer bacteria than the control groups.

Recommended Reading

Baer, Randall and Vicki. *The Crystal Connection.* New York: Harper & Row, 1986. In-depth study of pyramidology.

Davidovits, Joseph, and Margie Morris. *The Pyramids: An Enigma Solved.* New York: Hippocrene Books, Inc., 1988. Insight into the possible discovery of how the great Pyramids were built.

Flanagan, G. Pat. *Pyramid Power and Beyond Pyramid Power.* Marina del Rey, CA: De Vorss & Co., 1973 & 1975.

Lemesurier, Peter. *The Great Pyramid Decoded.* New York: Element Books, 1985. Pictures and technical material for the serious searcher.

Schul, Bill, and Ed Pettit. *The Psychic Power of Pyramids.* New York: Fawcett, 1976. A spiritual look.

Schul, Bill, and Ed Pettit. *Pyramid Power: A New Reality.* Walpole, NH: Stillpoint Publishing, 1987. New insights.

Stark, Norman. *The First Practical Pyramid Book.* Kansas City, MO: Sheed Andrews & McMeel, Inc., 1977. Easy instruction.

Reincarnation

Reincarnation

> *REINCARNATION assumes belief in the eternity of the soul. It means, literally, "in the flesh again." The word signifies the progression of the soul or life essence from the non-physical to the physical body, repetitively.*

A recent Gallup poll reports that one in four people in the United States believes in Reincarnation. That's an amazing 55 million people! It is a popular concept in part because it attempts to deal with the desire for continuity in one's life and the immortality of life itself.

The concept that a soul takes on a new physical form after death is not new. In fact, the *Catholic Encyclopedia* notes that it was once an integral part of Christian teachings. During an Ecumenical Council meeting (The Council of Nicea) in 553 A.D., the Catholic Church voted to strike the theory of Reincarnation from church dogma. The purpose of deleting this teaching was to unify the Church's power and authority over the lives of its followers.

There are as many variations to the theory of Reincarnation as there are off-shoots of major religions. The ancient Hindus believed one could regress on the path of Reincarnation and transmigrate to animal form; however, most people who accept Reincarnation today do not share this belief. It is more commonly felt the purpose of Reincarnation is to progress or evolve into higher and higher life forms.

Theosophists theorize that one can choose his or her incarnation. Metaphysical philosophy goes so far as to hold that one chooses his or her parents, surroundings, and handicaps — a choice which is not remembered in the current life. Reincarnationists believe this memory lapse is a necessity. One faces a difficult enough task coping with the depth of experience encountered in a single lifetime — memory of the experience of all lifetimes would interfere with the lessons learned *now*. However, it is thought that deja vu (see DEJA VU) is a glimmer of such memory.

Whether by personal choice or higher design, the lessons learned in one life's experience are presumed to carry over to the next, making each new life richer than the last. In this manner, a life sadly cut short in one incarnation can be redeemed in the next. Reincarnation is often thought to work within the law of karma (see KARMA) or cause and effect. In this way "what you sow, so shall you reap" life after life after life.

In his famous book, *The Prophet*, Kahlil Gibran shares his acceptance of Reincarnation:

> *Yes, I shall return with the time, and though death may hide me and the greater silence enfold me,... A little while, a moment of rest upon the wind, and another woman shall bear me.*

The great psychic Edgar Cayce (1877-1945), known as the "sleeping prophet," (1877-1945) suggests our soul's ultimate destination through Reincarnation is unification with God:

> *The cosmic plan for the soul's return involves cycles of experience, including multiple earth lives as well as periods of learning in other realms and planes of consciousness. These cycles continue until we return to a full consciousness of our spiritual source.*

Voltaire, when he looked at the theory of Reincarnation, said, "Being born twice is no more remarkable than being born once."

Research in hypnosis regression (see HYPNOSIS/HYPNOTHERAPY) supports the concept of Reincarnation by documenting cases in which the subject recalls, in verifiable detail, incidents of what are apparently previous lives. One such case is that of a woman with no knowledge of American history who lived in Germany in 1953. Under hypnosis, she related the detailed story of her experience with the "Donner Party," a wagon train trapped at Adler Creek in the American frontier during a winter storm of 1846. Historical records clearly verify the accuracy of her account.

One theory posits that some individuals, couples, and groups of people are reborn into the same time frame in order to evolve together. Dick Sutphen's, *You Were Born Again to be Together*, discusses the concept that in the nonphysical dimension before birth two or more people may agree to come together in the physical plane — as a family or in a close group or organization. It is thought that anyone about whom a person feels strongly (positively or negatively) may be someone with whom they have shared a past life or lives.

Recommended Reading

Fiore, Edith. *You Have Been Here Before.* New York: Ballantine Books, 1978. A psychologist looks at past lives.

Montgomery, Ruth. *Here & Hereafter.* New York: Coward-McCann, Inc., 1968. Entertaining.

Steiger, Francie and Brad. *Discover Your Own Past Lives.* New York: Dell Publishing, 1981. Technique book for remembering past lives.

Stevenson, Ian. *Twenty Cases Suggestive of Reincarnation.* New York: American Society for Psychical Research, 1966. Research and documentation on Reincarnation world wide.

Whitton, Joel, and Joe Fisher. *Life Between Life.* New York: Doubleday & Co., Inc., 1986.

Woolger, Roger. *Other Lives, Other Selves.* New York: Doubleday & Co., Inc., 1988. Past life therapy techniques.

Soul/Spirit

> *SOUL and SPIRIT are interchangeable words which describe the unique presence within every human or other organism expressed in the physical world. The Soul is the spiritual counterpart to one's material body.*

We each possess a physical, mental, and spiritual body. The spiritual body is one's Soul or personal Spirit. It is the lens of the Higher-Self (see HIGHER-SELF). This spiritual essence is reported to rise to the "white light" during a near-death-experience.

The Soul exists independently of the physical body and survives bodily death. The channeled entity Emmanuel tells us of the realms of spirit:

> *Give yourselves permission,*
> *at this very moment,*
> *to touch the world of spirit....*
> *Sigh into it.*
> *Your mind does not know the way*
> *Your heart has already been there.*
> *And your soul has never left it.*
> *Welcome home.*

Recommended Reading

Dossey, Larry M.D. *Recovering the Soul: A Scientific and Spiritual Search.* New York: Bantam Books, 1989.

Hopper, Darlene. *Direct from Spirit.* Malibu, CA: Valley of the Sun Publishing, 1983.

Jung, C.G. *Modern Man in Search of Soul.* New York: Harvest/HBJ, 1955. A soul-searching book.

Rodegast, Pat, and Judith Stanton. *Emmanuel's Book: A Manual for Living Comfortably in the Cosmos,* and *Emmanuel's Book II.* New York: Some Friends of Emmanuel and Bantam Books, 1985 and 1989. Sensitive and self-loving truths.

Spiritual/Religious

> SPIRITUAL *refers to that aspect surrounding the*
> *spirit, or the unseen nature of existence.*

> RELIGIOUS *refers to the aspect of devotion to a*
> *certain way of thinking, believing, and acting.*

Since the beginning of time, humanity has sought to understand its role in the infinite universe. Every so often an Avatar (see PROPHET/AVATAR) has incarnated into the physical world to guide our understanding and to share light with us. The wisdom of these spiritually advanced souls has formed the many organized religions of today. Religion is a way of trying to preserve the valuable Spiritual systems (meditation, prayer, yoga, ritual) and to keep alive the guidance of highly evolved prophets. Yet, in this New Age, large numbers of people are making the shift from following Religious authority to taking responsibility for their own growth and Spiritual development.

More and more people are pursuing an eclectic Spiritual journey in seeking awareness of their personal relationship with the Higher Power. They listen to the intuitive whispers from within and sort through the wealth of information contained in the world's many different religions to find that which speaks to *their* hearts.

Many individuals have found the rituals and ceremonies of fundamental religions have failed them. This growing number of people acknowledge that some religions use feelings of duty, obligation, righteousness, superiority, guilt and dualistic concepts like good/evil, heaven/hell to manipulate their personal power (see PERSONAL POWER). Also, the earliest teachings of many faiths have become distorted through repeated translations and reforms in organizing the religion. Peter Russell, the author of *The Global Brain,* likened this distortion to "a photocopy of a photocopy of a photocopy. With each copy the image becomes progressively more blurred."

The glorious dimension of spirit experienced by the spiritual Masters lies beyond the words. An enlightened soul may try to give us a glimpse of this ever-expanding realm, but their original message is often convoluted by humankind's limited understanding of true Spiritual awakening. Catholic theologian Anthony Padovano maintains that faith is not dying in the West; it is merely moving inside. Reverend Terry Cole-Whittaker said it this way when she addressed the UCORS Congress in 1982: "The only religion that will survive is a 'no religion, religion,' which will encourage one's own inner Spiritual exploration."

Recommended Reading

Crossen, Kendra, editor. *The Encyclopedia of Eastern Philosophy and Religion.* Boston, MA: Shambhala, 1988. "A complete survey of the teachers, traditions, and literature of Asian wisdom."

Fields, Rick, with Peggy Taylor, Rex Weyler, and Rick Ingrasci. *Chop Wood, Carry Water: A Guide to Finding Spiritual Fulfillment in Everyday Life.* Los Angeles, CA: J.P. Tarcher, Inc., 1984.

Huxley, Aldous. *The Perennial Philosophy.* New York: Harper & Row, 1970.

James, William. *The Varieties of Religious Experience.* New York: Macmillan, 1961. Topics include repentance, the mystic experience, saintliness, and the hopes of reward and fears of punishment.

Roberts, Bernadette. *The Experience of No-Self.* Boston, MA: Shambhala, 1982. Spiritual awakening through the loss-of-self as described in Christian mystical literature.

Smith, Huston. *The Religions of Man.* New York: Harper & Row, 1956. Informative and well written.

Spiritual Emergence Network, California Institute of Transpersonal Psychology, 250 Oak Grove Ave., Menlo Park, CA 94025. (415) 327-2776. An international "hot line" for individuals in psychic or spiritual crisis.

T'ai Chi

T'AI CHI is a form of Taoist movement meditation.

The lesson in T'ai Chi meditation (see MEDITATION) is to still the mind, to shift the awareness from consciousness to that of the intuitive. This form of silencing the mind includes slow-motion-like body movements which are learned by repeating them over and over. People of all ages can develop this meditative art form. The rhythmical movements bring peace of mind and activate the "chi" energy, the vital breath within man/woman. By the regular practice of T'ai Chi, one can release this chi energy thereby combating physical illness and emotional depression.

In the Chinese tradition, T'ai Chi follows the natural flow of divine energy:

> *Those who flow as life flows*
> *Know they need no other force,*
> *They feel no wear, they feel no tear,*
> *They need no mending, no repair.*

Recommended Reading

Liang, T.T. *T'ai Chi Ch'uan for Health and Self-Defense.* New York: Random House, Inc., 1977.

Cook, Robert. *Tai Chi Workout.* San Francisco: Creative Consultants International. Video workout.

Delza, Sophia. *T'ai Chi Ch'uan.* New York: Simon & Schuster, Inc., 1974. Guidebook.

Tarot/Runes

TAROT Cards and RUNES (small engraved stones) are used to encounter the Higher-Self to help direct the user toward the inner choices which determine the future.

Tarot Cards and the tablets of Runes are sources of guidance in the never-ending process of "self-change." They each have their specific ways to help guide and direct the user to that place of harmony surrounding what may be an unsettling situation. Tarot Cards have been more openly talked about in our culture than the Runic philosophy. Tarot "readings" are quite common at fairs and psychic events nationwide. However, the interpretation of Tarot must be found within the user — for they speak to the individual who questions for Higher Guidance. This is also true of the Runic Oracle.

A Tarot deck consists of seventy-eight pictorial cards which are divided into four suits; Swords (sometimes called Crystals), Batons or Wands, Cups or Coupes, and Pentacles or Worlds. Included are also the twenty-two "major arcana," principal cards which correspond to the branches found on the Tree of Life of the Caballah. The regular use of Tarot stimulates the conscious and subconscious reactions to symbolic or archetypal symbols (see ARCHETYPAL SYMBOLS). Each of these cards depicts the holistic psychology of the personality — mental, physical, and spiritual — to unravel a counsel found beyond words.

The Runes are small engraved stones, twenty-five in all, which also stimulate the reactions of the conscious and subconscious mind. They have been compared to the ancient Chinese "I Ching" (see I CHING). Originated by the Vikings, the Runes depict hieroglyphic forms of communication instead of pictures. Each tablet or stone signifies an individual path, or perhaps a bridge, to the Higher Knowing Self. They act as a catalyst to guide one to the inner whispers of divine order.

Recommended Reading

Blum, Ralph. *The Book of Runes.* New York: St. Martin's Press, 1987. This is a complete book with Runic tablets.

Dolphin, Deon. *Rune Magic: The Celtic Runes as a Tool for Personal Transformation.* North Hollywood, CA: Newcastle Publishing Co., Inc., 1987. How Runes may be used as a contemporary oracle.

Haich, Elisabeth. *The Wisdom of the Tarot.* New York: Aurora Press, 1975.

Metzner, Ralph. *Maps of Consciousness.* New York: The Macmillan Co., 1972.

Wanless, James. *Voyager Guidebook.* Carmel, CA: Merrill-West Publishing, 1986. Tarot instruction book and symbolic deck of cards to spur the imagination.

Third Eye

> *The THIRD EYE refers to the sixth chakra center, the "mind's eye."*

The chakra energy centers (see CHAKRA) are located in a straight vertical line beginning with the root, or base chakra and culminating at the top of the head or crown. The Third Eye chakra is the sixth energy wheel situated in the middle of the forehead between the eyebrows. This energy center activates the intuitive or spiritual awareness. In yoga meditation (see MEDITATION) one focuses (with eyes closed) all conscious awareness upon this area to stimulate the spirit and promote peace of mind. The use of the Third Eye brings added understanding, much as reading between the lines or beyond the words gives us added insight to their meaning.

In ancient art and literature the Third Eye chakra is open and many times portrayed with an image of a human eye, an open lotus flower, or crystal gem stone displayed at the center. Rene Descartes and others called this sixth chakra the "seat of the soul." Practice and concentration using the Third Eye center can result in flashes of spiritual insight and intuitive mystical knowledge.

Recommended Reading

Baker, Douglas. *The Opening of the Third Eye.* New York: Samuel Weiser, 1977.

Samuels, Mike. *Seeing With the Mind's Eye.* New York: Random House, Inc., 1976. Visualizations and uses of intuition.

Yoga

YOGA is a system of living originating from the Eastern philosophy of Hinduism. American culture usually associates the term Yoga with one aspect of this system which focuses on the techniques and disciplines of certain body postures. This type of Yoga is called Hatha Yoga.

The word Yoga comes from Sanskrit, its root meaning is "union" or "join." This very aptly describes the practice of Yoga — a union or joining with the three aspects of body, mind, and spirit.

Hatha Yoga is just one path in the Yoga system and is a form of mind/body centering for relaxation and fitness. The practice of Hatha Yoga entails centering or calming the mind in a meditative state while undergoing different body stances, or postures, to ensure body flexibility and peace of mind. In this way, one undergoes the yogic way of holistic health (see HOLISM/HOLISTIC HEALTH).

Yoga, if practiced with discipline, can become the avenue necessary for total "integration" of the body, mind, and spirit. Written in a sacred Hindu story, the *Bhagavad Gita*, the following passage is found:

Having mastered the body by means of the Yogic teachings, so that it becomes a fit habitation for the soul; having the senses, emotions, and mind under control, the wise person discards the worn-out sheaths of desire, fear, and confusion and passes into the state of enlightenment and freedom.

The freedom from fear and confusion leads to the Light — the "en-lightenment" — one is seeking while on the journey through the Yoga system. By becoming enlightened, one discards old negative patterns and beliefs and disengages from using the emotions for personal desire. The yogic way of attuning to the body, mind and spirit is an ancient ritual. Its use can also be found at the begining of Christianity when "secret meditation" was taught to monks.

Recommended Reading

Haich, Elisabeth. *The Day With Yoga.* New York: Aurora Press. Small book containing quotations to attune to the cosmic vibrations of each day.

Hittleman, Richard. *Guide to Yoga Meditation.* New York: Bantam.

Hittleman, Richard. *Introduction to Yoga.* New York: Bantam.

Hittleman, Richard. *30 Day Yoga Meditation.* New York: Bantam.

Hittleman, Richard. *The Eight Steps to Health and Peace.* New York: Bantam. All these and others by same author are simple yet informative works on the yogic system.

Iyengar, B. *Light on Yoga.* New York: Schocken Books, 1977.

Rama, Swami, Rudolph Ballentine, and Swami Ajaya. *Yoga & Psychotherapy: The Evolution of Consciousness.* Honesdale, PA: Himalayan Institute, 1976. In-depth study of the Yoga system and its relation to human consciousness.

Tobias, Maxine, and Mary Stewart. *Stretch & Relax.* Arizona: The Body Press, 1985. Pictorial pages of exercises.

Woods, Ernest E. *Yoga.* New York: Penguin Books, 1968. Good postures and directions.

Future Visions

"We're all the sons of God, or children of the Is, or ideas of the Mind, or however else you want to say it...."
Yeah, the whole motion of our time is from the material toward the spiritual....slow as it is, it's still a pretty huge motion."

Richard Bach, *Illusions*

Awakening/Enlightenment/Illumination

AWAKENING, ENLIGHTENMENT, ILLUMINA-TION are words that attempt to describe spontaneous contact with ultimate Truth. This experience lies beyond ordinary consciousness and touches intuitive intelligence or the "Buddha in all things."

Illumination/Enlightenment is a rare phenomenon. It is the Awakening from the dream that one is separate from All That Is. In Buddhism, this state of total liberation is call *nirvana* and the opening of the third eye (see THIRD EYE) to this Illumination is named *satori*. Enlightenment moves one beyond a dualistic illusion to a direct transpersonal experience of unity with the divinity of the universe.

The ancient masters taught that our original nature is of the Enlightened Buddha or Christ, and that we have just forgotten this truth. Hazrat Inayat Khan wrote that the transformative call of Enlightenment rings clearly to those whose moment of awakening has arrived, and is a lullaby for those who must still sleep. Zen Buddhists say you are already enlightened; all you have to do is wake up to the fact.

Illumination jolts one from the "sleep-walking" state of ordinary consciousness and brings with it the transcendent wisdom of the impermanence of material reality. The religious doctrine of the Avatamska Sutra teaches that for those who have become Enlightened the boundaries of individuality fade as we see through our self-imposed limitations.

Enlightenment penetrates appearances, beyond this dance of holographic illusion (see ILLUSION/HOLOGRAM) we call life. It is a direct intuitive experience of the Self. In his book, *What We May Be,* Piero Ferrucci shares the work of Roberto Assagioli — creator of the field of psychology known as psychosynthesis (see PSYCHOSYNTHESIS) — and his study of a number of illuminations. He quotes Dr. Assagioli's findings as follows:

An inner perception of light which in certain cases is so intense as to be described as a dazzling glory and an impression of fire. It is from these characteristics that the term "illumination" has arisen,...

A sense of oneness with the whole.... Feelings of joy, of peace, of love,...rising above the "flux of becoming," above past, present, and future. The realization of the Eternal Now and of the essential permanence, indestructibility, and immortality of one's own spiritual Self, of the Center of one's being.

An urge to express — to communicate to others — the illumination, to share this precious treasure, and a sense of compassionate love for those still wandering and suffering in darkness and illusion.

Fifty-two supernormal powers, called *siddhis* in yogic philosophy, are said to accompany Enlightenment. These powers range from clairvoyance, telepathy, levitation, walking on water, to being in two places at once. Buddha, Christ, Krishna, St. Theresa of Avila, St. John of the Cross, Catherine of Sienna, and Joseph of Copertino (among others) were said to be endowed with powers to perform these "miracles" (see MIRACLES).

Jesus claimed that the powers to manipulate reality were available to everyone: "You shall be able to do all these things and more." The word "Christ" was added to the name of Jesus because *Christ* literally means "the Illumined one." Recognizing that these abilities are a sign of spiritual Enlightenment, the Roman Catholic Church made the performance of miracles a prerequisite for official canonization.

Recommended Reading

Bucke, Richard M. *Cosmic Consciousness.* New York: Dutton, 1923. Exceptional individuals through history who were gifted with the power of transcendent realization.

Golas, Thaddeus. *The Lazy Man's Guide to Enlightenment.* New York: Bantam Books, 1972.

Tart, Charles. *Waking Up: Overcoming the Obstacles to Human Potential.* Boston, MA: Shambhala Publications, 1986.

White, John. *What is Enlightenment?* Los Angeles: J.P. Tarcher, Inc., 1984. Fifteen highly respected spiritual teachers (including Sri Aurobindo, Krishnamurti, Meher Baba, Ken Wilber, and Huston Smith) discuss the many aspects of Enlightenment.

Centers of Light/New Age Communities

CENTERS OF LIGHT and NEW AGE COM-MUNITIES are composed of people who choose to express their individuality in a group which is concerned with New Age concepts and transformative principles.

One example of a New Age Community is Findhorn in Scotland. It began when three people became aware of humanity's imbalanced relationship to the Nature World of the Devas (see DEVAS/ELEMEN-TALS). As their garden grew so did the number of persons in the community. With this rapid growth came the realization that the transformation in their remarkable garden was a metaphor for the personal transformative flowering occurring among the members of the group. The spiritual principles of unity and harmony put to use in their relationship with the garden were also evolving their relationships to one another.

Like Findhorn, the object of a New Age Community is for people to live in cooperation with nature and with each other in a lifestyle that increases one's awareness. These communities are challenged to create synergistic systems of leadership, patterns of government, economic security, and innovative approaches to relationships and child-rearing. They must deal with the physical and material, as well as the metaphysical and spiritual concerns of their members.

Another New Age Community is Harbin Hot Springs in Northern California. This Light Center, founded in 1972, is where an average of 130 residents play and live together. Harbin provides retreat and conference facilities, as well as hot, warm and cold mineral springs, for public enjoyment. One young resident expressed her feelings about living in a New Age Community this way, "I like the sense of community and mutual support. I am never really alone, there's always someone I can talk to — there are always friends around."

A New Age Community is not a place in which to *hide* oneself, but in which to find *more* of oneself and in that process to explore creative alternatives in living. These communities of like-minded individuals form an emerging new world view of cooperation and global peace. Underlying it all is a deep human memory of oneness, and thus, a desire for a holistic relationship with others. Many of the larger Centers of Light, such as Auroville, India; Another Place, New England; Arcosanti, Arizona; and Findhorn, Scotland also network (see NETWORKING) with each other to expand their sense of *world* community.

Recommended Reading

The Findhorn Community. *Faces of Findhorn: Images of a Planetary Family.* New York: Harper & Row, 1980. A look inside the hearts and minds of Findhorn.

Harbin Springs Publishing. *The New Age Community Guidebook: Alternative Choices in Lifestyles.* Middletown, CA: Harbin Springs Publishing, 1989. A must for anyone interested in joining a community.

Hawken, Paul. *Findhorn: A Center of Light.* San Francisco: Tao Publishing, 1974.

McLaughlin, Corinne, and Gordon Davidson. *Builders of the Dawn: Community Lifestyles in a Changing World.* Shutesbury, MA: Sirius Publications, 1988. Realistic observations of communal living in more than 150 communities around the world.

Peck, M. Scott, M.D. *The Different Drum: Community Making and Peace.* New York: Simon & Schuster, Inc., 1987. Fascinating stories and case histories fill this warm and inspiring book.

Harbin Hot Springs, a New Age Community and retreat center offering educational facilities, conference buildings, natural mineral pools, and a spiritual space for self-healing and renewal. For information write: Harbin Hot Springs, P.O. Box 82, Middletown, CA 95461. (707) 987-2477 or (800) 622-2477 in Northern California.

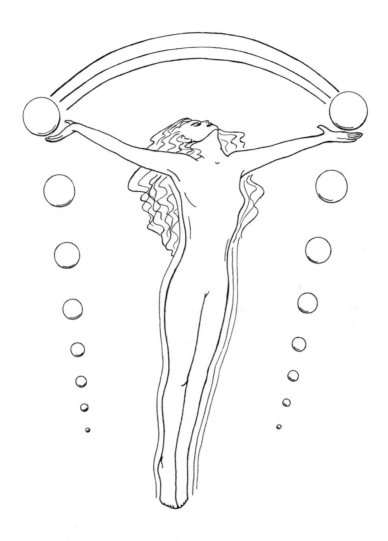

Cosmic Consciousness

Cosmic Consciousness

COSMIC CONSCIOUSNESS is that spontaneous glimpse of an experience of Oneness, timelessness, perfection, and truth which is infinite awareness.

Cosmic Consciousness lies beyond words, self-awareness or self-consciousness. It is pure awareness, order, knowledge, and spirit. Cosmic consciousness is divine love creating and unfolding. It is infinite and timeless. It is also a part of all of us and a part of every *thing*.

This state of pure awareness, or Cosmic Consciousness, can be attained; however, few people in our evolutionary history have lived in it continually. Avatar Meher Baba, calls this state of awareness, "God-realisation." He writes:

God-realisation is a unique state of consciousness. It is different from all the other states of consciousness because all the other states of consciousness are experienced through the medium of the individual mind; whereas the state of God-realisation is in no way dependent upon the individual mind or any other medium.

In an altered state of consciousness (see ALTERED STATES OF CONSCIOUSNESS) one might catch a glimpse of Cosmic Consciousness.

This realization of Oneness and Unity (see UNITY/ONENESS) comes perhaps to few physical beings, but teaches us that there are no "others" — only *us* together, as a unit of love and infinite spirit.

The term Cosmic Consciousness has been synonymous with other words such as Universal Subconscious Mind or Cosmic Awareness. Whatever you label it, Cosmic Consciousness remains synonymous with Divine Love.

Recommended Reading

Anderson,U.S. *Three Magic Words*. North Hollywood, CA: Wilshire Book Co., CA, 1976.

Burke, Richard M. *Cosmic Consciousness.* Secaucus, NJ: Citadel Press, 1984. Study of evolution of the human mind.

Keyes, Ken. *Handbook to Higher Consciousness.* Coos Bay, OR: Love Line Books, 1978. Investigates the seven levels of consciousness, arriving at the Center of Cosmic Consciousness.

Meher Baba. *Discourses Vol. II.* CA: Kingsport Press, 1967.

Rivers, Gloria. *Cosmic Consciousness: The Highway to Wholeness.* Portland, OR: Temple Publishers, 1987.

Divine Order

> *DIVINE ORDER is a belief in the underlying harmony and order in our universe.*

One windy evening a nameless philosopher looked up at the night sky and said, "The stars are in their heaven and everything is right with the world." If not for Divine Order, these words would never have been uttered; planets would cease to rotate around the sun; constellations would collide; and the cosmos would probably wobble. Our personal worlds are directed by Divine Order as well. In *Emmanuel's Book*, channeled by Pat Rodegast, Emmanuel states:

> *In your concept of the cosmos,*
> *be aware of the stability*
> *that allows for individual chaos.*

Nothing random lives in the universe. Divine Order operates to bring all life into its highest Light and karmic balance. Even that which appears in disorder has purpose. "Letting go and letting God" affirms the universal principle (see UNIVERSAL LAWS/PRINCIPLES) of Divine Order and releases one's small picture of "how things should be" to the realization of a Higher Order.

Recommended Reading

Bohm, David, and F. David Peat. *Science, Order, and Creativity*. New York: Bantam Books, 1987.

Hoff, Benjamin. *The Tao of Pooh*. New York: Penguin Books, 1982. Enchanting.

Rodegast, Pat, and Judith Stanton. *Emmanuel's Book: A Manual for Living Comfortably in the Cosmos*. New York: Some Friends of Emmanuel and Bantam Books, 1985. Expresses the elegant Divine Order of the universe.

Rodegast, Pat, and Judith Stanton. *Emmanuel's Book II*. New York: Some Friends of Emmanuel and Bantam Books, 1989.

Inner Voice/Whispers

> *The INNER VOICE, or the proverbial "still small voice within," is an inward message from one's Higher-Self or inner advisor.*

> *WHISPERS are outward signs of guidance from one's Higher-Self which may take a variety of forms.*

We each possess an inherent guidance system made up of gentle impulses from within, such as intuition, an Inner Voice, dream messages, and synchronicities (see Individual Headings). These inner and outer communications are said to originate from one's Higher-Self (see HIGHER-SELF).

Access to the voice of one's Higher-Self is often clearest during a quiet moment or meditation. This Inner Voice is not to be confused with voices originating from the inner child, critical parent, or ego. Unlike one's Higher-Self, these voices often use judgmental phrases and self-serving language. With the practice of *conscious* inner-listening, one can learn to identify the Higher-Self's positive guidance.

Whispers are another form of guidance from your Higher-Self that occur when your outer world is trying to tell you something. Your reality is "Whispering" to you, for instance, when you find yourself deep in thought about a particular problem in your life and suddenly see a bumper sticker, road sign, or open a newspaper that in some way clearly answers that problem. Your Higher-Self may Whisper advice when you flick on the television set or radio just as it is discussing the pros and cons of a situation you were questioning the moment before. Or, an off-handed remark by a total stranger may hold the precise answer you are seeking.

Our entire reality is constantly nudging us toward greater awareness and spiritual growth. A pain in the neck, a dream, the dynamics of a personal relationship, all interactions with one's environment are messages from the Higher-Self. If one does not pay attention to these messages or is not listening to the Inner Voices, the Whispers will become louder and louder. They could turn into "shouts of reality" such as illness, job loss, broken relationships, or other disruptions. These growth lessons through crisis persist until a conscious change is made. However, we can *choose* to grow through inner-listening, paying attention to our reality, and learning through the loving Whispers that surround us each moment.

Recommended Reading

Gittner, Louis. *Listen - Listen - Listen.* WA: Louis Foundation, 1980. Stuffed with spiritual truth to develop the inner-listening ear.

Lazaris. *The Sacred Journey: You and Your Higher Self.* Palm Beach, FL: NPN Publishing, Inc., 1987. Cosmic joy in book form.

Long, Mildred. *Listen to the Silence.* Marina del Rey, CA: DeVorss & Co., 1970.

Light

LIGHT ... a spark of Universal Enlightenment.

The capitalized word, Light, is being used in the New Age to represent an aspect of the Divine Being. This term is found in literature and conversations relating the significant relationship between the Oneness of the universe (see UNITY/ONENESS) and our individual humanness.

There have been several books recently published which contain the word Light in the title: *Dancing in the Light, Living in the Light, Seeds of Light.* However, we cannot assume "Light" is used in the same context every time it is printed.

In their book, *Higher Creativity*, the authors explore the vital role of Light in ancient religions and modern science:

> *To find inspired statements regarding the nature of light and its connection to the god-head and the origin of the cosmos, we need only turn to Genesis, in which the primary act of creation began with light. In the Tibetan Book of the Dead, the "clear light of the void" is discussed as the fundamental "substance" of which the universe and mankind are made. The Hindu Bhagavad Gita mentions "the splendor of a thousand suns..."*

Our use of the word-symbol, Light, reminds us of our origin as children of the Creator, who commanded at the beginning of time, "Let there be Light."

Recommended Reading

Bova, Ben. *The Beauty of Light.* New York: John Wiley & Sons, Inc., 1988. Scientific and en-Lightening.

Gawain, Shakti. *Living in the Light.* San Rafael, CA: New World Library, 1986.

Huffines, LaUna. *Bridge of Light: Tools of Light for Spiritual Transformation.* Tiburon, CA: H.J. Kramer, Inc., 1989. Visualizations and healing systems to create bridges of Light in one's life.

Metzner, Ralph. *Opening to Inner Light: The Transformation of Human Nature & Consciousness.* Los Angeles: J.P. Tarcher, 1986.

Rengel, Peter. *Seeds of Light.* Tiburon, CA: H.J. Kramer, Inc., 1987. A collection of inspirational quotes to seed Light into the soul.

Wind, Wabun, and Anderson Reed. *Lightseeds.* New York: Prentice-Hall Press, 1988.

Networking

NETWORKING is an interweaving of resources and access to information by like-minded people.

Networking is not new, it has been around since time immemorial. Alcoholics Anonymous has long used positive support Networking as a basis for mutual self-help. Gandhi realized the power of Networks which he called, "grouping unities," to bring India to independence. Street gangs and the Mafia could also be considered Networks because they are "antidotes to alienation." However, Networks are taking on new meaning as we approach the end of the twentieth century and they are rapidly proliferating.

Marilyn Ferguson, author of *The Aquarian Conspiracy,* writes:

Once you have seen the power inherent in human alignment, you cannot think about the future in old terms.... This spiraling linkage — individuals with each other, groups with groups — is like a great resistance movement, an underground in an occupied country on the eve of liberation. Power is changing hands, from dying hierarchies to living networks.

Alfred Katz, organizer of an international conference to form Mutual Aid Networks, feels that networks are a social impulse toward the resistance to bureaucratic trends in the close of this twentieth century. Networks seek to multiply resources in a noncompetitive, cooperative, flexible, self-organizing manner. The result of these clustering groups and grapevines is greater mutual benefit, personal power (see PERSONAL POWER) and a sense of community.

Today, Networks are shifting the power from institutionalized medicine to Holistic Health methods which encourage personal responsibility. Also, economic and political power is being rechanneled by cooperative buying and social protest. The Network link of computers and concern by individuals has found its way into most facets of human experience. Networking is helping in many diverse areas, such as: shared child-care, programs for the handicapped; missing persons bureaus; drug, child, and animal abuse prevention programs; personal growth and social transformation; psychological well-beingness advocates; environmentalists; and peace through nuclear freeze groups.

Thousands of publications and Networking organizations revolve specifically around "new paradigm" experiences (see PARADIGM SHIFT). They offer fraternity and celebration to millions of persons involved in a global transformative movement. Barbara Marx Hubbard once called Networking "supra-sex" — an almost sensual affinity with like-minded others who share the New Age vision. This kinship is promoting change in our social and political structures based on spiritual values and collective vision.

A microcosmic view (see MICROCOSM/MACROCOSM) of this Networking system has been revealed by quantum physicists in their exploration of the subatomic world. They have discovered that the material universe is composed of dynamic patterns of integral systems and Networking interactions. The ground-core of life is an interweaving of movement toward greater cooperation, communication, and awareness. Human Networking is a *macrocosmic* expression of the unifying principle that we are not isolated entities, but part of a greater inseparable Network of consciousness.

Recommended Readings

Lipnack, Jessica, and Jeffrey Stamps. *The Networking Book.* New York: Routledge and Kegan Paul, Inc., 1986. Thousands of positive Networks explored, includes a Network directory.

New Age

> *The NEW AGE is an era in our developmental evolu-*
> *tion — a shift in paradigms of consciousness.*

"As you grow weary of wondering when the New Age will begin, you will decide it already did!" This quote from a channeled friend named Lazaris accurately describes the onset of the New Age — it has already begun. Just as it may be difficult to pinpoint exactly when the Age of Technology or the Renaissance began, we cannot say the exact year the New Age started; however, we can look to our human behavioral changes and growth patterns to recognize that a new state of mind has seeded itself within humanity.

The New Age is a state of expanding consciousness within the world. It cannot be defined as a particular movement, religion, science, type of therapy, technique for transcendence, or any other individual process or philosophy because the New Age encompasses all of these but still maintains its own broad definition. To label the New Age one or a combination of many tools, techniques, or philosophies would reduce the true evolutionary meaning of this era to a limited tunnel vision perspective.

When we look to the stars for a definition, we find the Age of Aquarius emerging from the Piscean Age. Poems, songs, and literature of all kinds are being written about this New Age unfolding before us — more accurately *within* us. The New Age brings with it an internal spiritual relationship, not a mere religion, rather an awareness or awakening of that "Something More." Along with this awareness comes the realization that each of us individually possesses the ability to control, create, and re-create our own reality; that "conscious creation" is possible and that personal reality is limited only by one's individual choices and decisions, thoughts and feelings, attitudes and beliefs. This gift of awareness is brought to us by the New Age.

In *The Final Choice*, Michael Grosso calls that "Something More" the "Mind at Large." He writes of the individual roles we play in the conscious creation for survival of our planet:

> *The good news is that a real psychospiritual force is awakening*
> *in the world today — an expression of Mind at Large, the*
> *guiding intelligence of Life itself. It draws its strength in part*

from individual minds, from what each of us does and thinks...
If we cast a cold eye on all high dreams and utopian visions,
we only abort the birth of the possible. But if we choose to
believe in the vision of a New Age, we may, thereby, hasten its
coming.

Sri Aurobindo, a mystic (see MYSTIC/MYSTICISM), writes of the unfolding New Age in a poem:

Our ideal is a new birth of humanity into the spirit;
our life must be a spiritually inspired effort
to create a body of action for the great new birth and crea-
tion.
Our ideal is not the spirituality that withdraws from
life
but the conquest of life by the power of the spirit.
It is to accept the world as an effort of manifestation
of the Divine,
but also to transform humanity
by a greater effort of manifestation than has yet been ac-
complished,
one in which the veil between man and God shall be
removed,
the divine manhood of which we are capable shall come to
birth
and our life shall be remolded in the truth and light
and power of the spirit.

Recommended Reading

Davis, Lola. *A Religion for the New Age.* New York: Coleman Publishing, 1983. A synthesis of a world philosophy for the New Age.

Ferguson, Marilyn. *The Aquarian Conspiracy.* Los Angeles: J.P. Tarcher, Inc., 1980. An overview of humanity's unfolding process in the New Age.

Grosso, Michael. *The Final Choice: Playing the Survival Game.* Walpole, NH: Stillpoint Publishing, 1986. A look at the conditions present for global change and healing in the New Age.

Harman, Willis. *Global Mind Change: The Promise of the Last Years of the Twentieth Century.* Indianapolis, IN: Knowledge Systems, Inc., 1988.

Lazaris. *The Sacred Journey: You and Your Higher Self.* Palm Beach, FL: NPN Publishing, Inc., 1987. Channeled guidance and inspiration for the New Age.

Trevelyan, Sir George. *A Vision of the Aquarian Age: The Emerging Spiritual World View.* Walpole, NH: Stillpoint Publishing, 1984. A visionary interprets the patterns of change in the New Age.

Paradigm Shift

> *A PARADIGM SHIFT is a dramatic change or a revolution of a dominant theoretical framework.*

The word Paradigm is derived from the Greek *paradigma,* which means pattern. The term "Paradigm Shift" was coined in 1962 by philosopher and science historian Thomas Kuhn, in his book *The Structure of Scientific Revolutions.* Kuhn explained that a Paradigm Shift occurs when a critical number of thinkers challenge a set of assumptions underlying a particular field of thought. A new framework begins to form which in turn influences our perceptions, values, and ways of thinking.

Paradigm Shifts do not occur with ease. New structure is often seen as threatening and is met with resistance, ridicule, and hostility. The old forms must lie fallen or failing for consensus to be broken and for change to take place. An established Paradigm of thought is discarded only when anomalies (irregular or contradictory evidence) accumulate and severely strain the old structure. Ultimately, a new perspective emerges when the status quo can no longer be preserved.

A classic example of a Paradigm Shift is the revolution in astronomy initiated by sixteenth century astronomer Nicolaus Copernicus. Copernicus challenged the Paradigm that the Earth was the center of the universe. This model, formulated by Greek astronomer Ptolemy around 140 A.D., remained virtually unchallenged for thirteen hundred years. Over the centuries more and more anomalies were uncovered that stressed this model. However, the church still claimed as heresy any view other than the Earth occupying the center of the universe. Several of those who openly supported the Copernican model were even burned at the stake. Fearing for his safety, Copernicus refused to publish his findings until late in his life.

The old Paradigm held fast through several more phases of discovery. Eighty years after Copernicus, Johannes Kepler, a German astronomer, came into possession of the astronomical observations made by Danish astronomer Tycho Brahe. Kepler theorized our sun-centered system, but his model was dismissed by the establishment. Next, Italian mathematician Galileo used the Dutch invention of the telescope to gather evidence for Kepler's model. University professors who felt threatened by these new discoveries united with the church to denounce Galileo for blasphemy. He was drawn before the Inquisition and forced to "abjure, curse, and detest" his "absurd" notion that the Earth moved around the sun. Finally, in 1687, Sir Isaac Newton shifted this Paradigm when he published his major work, the *Principia Mathematica* which provided further evidence for Kepler's theories. Today we still hold to this Paradigm of thought and have proven the Earth does indeed circle the sun.

Kuhn outlined five stages which generally characterize a Paradigm Shift: 1) Anomalies arise which challenge the present Paradigm. These contradictions are either incorporated in the present model or discounted. 2) Evidence continues to build against the old Paradigm and cannot be explained away. 3) This leads to the formulation of a new Paradigm to explain the new evidence. 4) Those attached to the old familiar Paradigm resist the change and this period of transition often leads to bitter struggle. 5) The final stage is acceptance of a new Paradigm. In this final stage, Kuhn believes that a larger perspective is not figured out, but instead, is suddenly seen as true.

Our history shows us dramatic Paradigm Shifts and leaps in our evolution through the discovery of fire, the wheel, language, and writing. More recently, we have discovered that the Earth only *appears* flat and revolutionary findings in our modern physics (see QUANTUM PHYSICS) testify that matter only *appears* solid. Our questioning has led us time and again to change our thinking and widen our perceptions. Just as the Renaissance, the Middle Ages, and the Industrial Age introduced new ways of seeing and experiencing the world around us, so too does the New Age bring us to a sudden liberation from old limits.

Our current materialistic world view is being challenged by recent findings in quantum physics, parapsychology and a rediscovery of mystic wisdom and perennial philosophy. As with any great revolution of change, the acceptance of new form requires patience and a melting of resistance before being adopted by the mainstream establishment. Inspired author of *The Aquarian Conspiracy*, Marilyn Ferguson, writes:

Revolutionary thinkers do not believe in single revolutions. They see change as a way of life.

Recommended Reading

Capra, Fritjof. *The Turning Point.* New York: Bantam Books, 1982. An optimistic, and hopefully accurate, account of the transforming Western worldview.

Ferguson, Marilyn. *The Aquarian Conspiracy.* Los Angeles: J.P. Tarcher, Inc., 1980.

Harman, Willis. *Global Mind Change.* Indianapolis, IN: Knowledge Systems, 1988. Explores the shifting Paradigm of the "Last Years of the Twentieth Century."

Harman, Willis. *An Incomplete Guide to the Future.* New York: W.W. Norton, 1979.

Kuhn, Thomas S. *The Structure of Scientific Revolutions.* Chicago: University of Chicago Press, 1970.

Wilber, Ken, editor. *The Holographic Paradigm and Other Paradoxes,* Boston, MA: Shambhala Publishing, 1988. Prominent scientists and thinkers explore the leading edge of science.

Personal Power

> *PERSONAL POWER is the process of facing, with an open heart and mind, the complex, unknown, ever-present experience of life.*

Personal Power is not about intimidation or power *over* others. It is about acknowledging and becoming in tune with the inexhaustible power from *within* yourself. Lazaris defines Personal Power as the ability and willingness to act. This ability to express your truest self and act upon your beliefs transforms a sense of victimhood and blame into Personal Power. One way to develop greater levels of Personal Power is to take total responsibility for your thoughts and actions. This requires courage, character, and trust in yourself. To fully *own* your beliefs means you no longer try to hide your honest feelings by blending like a chameleon into the changing colors of the latest accepted attitudes.

There are many words and concepts now bandied about in this emerging New Age — terms such as integrity, self-love, impact, responsibility, self-esteem and self-worth, and Personal Power. These words are being redefined in light of the current paradigm shift (see PARADIGM SHIFT). Perhaps we can best understand these terms not in the context of an attainable end result, but as an on-going process of transformative thought. These ideals are continually evolving as *we* evolve.

Recommended Reading

Campbell, Joseph. *The Hero with a Thousand Faces.* Princeton, NJ: Princeton University Press, 1968. Campbell's most important single work on mythology and Power.

Castaneda, Carlos. *Tales of Power.* New York: Pocket Books, 1974.

Cole-Whittaker, Terrry. *Love and Power in a World Without Limits: A Woman's Guide to the Goddess Within.* New York: Harper & Row Publishing, Inc., 1989.

Eknath, Easwaran. *Gandhi the Man.* Petaluma, CA: Nilgiri Press, 1973. The Story of how Gandhi transformed himself from an awkward teenager without a purpose to a powerful man who could take moral issue with the largest empire in the world — and win.

Keyes, Penny, and Ken Keyes, Jr. *Gathering Power Through Insight and Love.* Coos Bay, OR: Love Line Books, 1986.

Macy, Joanna. *Despair and Personal Power in the Nuclear Age.* Philadelphia, PA: New Society Publishers, 1983.

Roman, Sanaya. *Personal Power through Awareness.* Tiburon, CA: H.J. Kramer Inc., 1986. Following a spiritual path to Personal Power.

Wing, R.L. *The Tao of Power.* New York: Doubleday, 1986. Lao Tzu's classic guide to leadership, influence, and excellence.

SPACESHIP — EARTH

Planetary Peace

Planetary Peace

PLANETARY PEACE is the result of a global mind-set which does not justify war as a means of settling human conflict.

John F. Kennedy said, "We must put an end to war or war will put an end to us." In our nuclear age these words could not ring more true. We are dangling precariously on the precipice of global destruction — our spaceship-earth cannot afford even one nuclear war. Nineteenth century Prussian strategist Von Clausewitz pointed out that war is an extension of state policy. As it stands, current governmental policy-making highlights economic considerations, distrust and hostility, and mass consumption of ever-increasing goods and energy. Somewhere far down the list, we vaguely recognize our suffering environment and the individual human being.

One major step toward Planetary Peace is to change national policies which continue to glorify war and view expansion of the arms race as "good for the economy." We, the people, have the power to withdraw legitimacy from war and alter the history of humankind. In our recent past, we have decided to no longer tolerate subjugation, torture, mutilation of women, child labor, and other human indignities. We can also say *no* to war.

Non-peace generally arises from disharmony between political ideologies, racial prejudices, religious views, economic concerns, or resource scarcity. Our world is presently operating at a very low level of synergy (see SYNERGY) with many of the above conflicts seemingly unresolvable. Because of this, we tolerate war, rationalize starvation, and close our eyes to the pludering of our planet's diminishing natural resources. Time is quickly running out for the survival of our species. A dramatic change or shift in the collective beliefs which have created our current self-destructive condition may be our only hope. In their book, *Higher Creativity,* Willis Harman and Howard Rheingold state:

Our interdependence and interconnectedness are making it clear that when there is mass poverty and starvation, the whole of the planet is ill. Only now do we have a growing group of people around the world who know that chronic mass starva-

tion cannot humanely be allowed to continue, and that it is intolerable to pass it on as a legacy generation after generation, in the ever-present threat of nuclear holocaust. These are people who know that deterrence was at best a stopgap whose time has passed, and that Star Wars-style defenses against nuclear weapons are a dangerous and expensive myth.

In this age of intellect-gone-wild, we keep finding new ways of misusing science. Our technology has led us to an unprecedented threat to all life on the planet. One does not need to be a scientist to realize a nuclear war would have no winner; it is absurd to spend over a billion dollars a day on a global arms race when we have already produced the nuclear equivalent of three tons of TNT for every man, woman, and child on Earth.

We are confronted with a crisis of meaning and a lack of environmental and human-centered values. However, with the end of the 1980's and the beginning of the last decade before the 21st Century, great strides towards freedom and human rights are being made. The falling of the Berlin Wall is a powerful symbol for this momentous time of change. Individually, we can each use this macrocosmic metaphor to ask ourselves: What is *my* personal Berlin Wall? What barriers within *me* have yet to fall?

Humanity is rich with latent potentialities: We have a desire for peace, a yearning to improve, a need for justice, and an innate creative intelligence. The authors of *Higher Creativity* suggest four steps we can each take toward bringing the vision of global peace into reality:

1. Say "no" to the insanity of tolerating war as a means of settling disputes. No longer justify widespread poverty, disease, starvation, or environmental degradation while allowing escalation of arms race expenditures.

2. Say "yes" to evolutionary transformation. Hold a vision of peace and regularly affirm that "Global peace is possible, and nothing less is tolerable."

3. "Do your inner work." Listen to your "deep intuition" as a guide to change inner beliefs which perpetuate non-peace in your personal life and in the world.

4. "Do your outer work." Work to actively shape humanity's future toward peace in whatever role or capacity you feel guided. A "fairness revolution" must begin with the beliefs and actions of each individual for a change to occur macrocosmically in the world.

Recommended Reading

Barnaby, Frank, general editor. *The Gaia Peace Atlas.* New York: Doubleday, 1988. A focused call to action.

Ferguson, Marilyn. *The Aquarian Conspiracy.* Los Angeles: J.P. Tarcher, Inc., 1980. A modern day bible of Planetary Peace.

Grosso, Michael. *The Final Choice.* Walpole, NH: Stillpoint Publishing, 1986.

Harman, Willis. *Global Mind Change.* Indianapolis, IN: Knowledge Systems, Inc., 1988. A welcome breath of clarity.

Harman, Willis, and Howard Rheingold. *Higher Creativity.* Los Angeles: J.P. Tarcher, Inc., 1984.

Russell, Peter. *The Global Brain.* Los Angeles: J.P. Tarcher, Inc., 1983. Fascinating speculations on the "evolutionary leap to planetary consciousness."

Schmookler, Andrew Bard. *Out of Weakness: Healing the Wounds that Drive Us to War.* New York; Bantam Books, 1988. Should be required reading for all top defense and foreign policy officials.

Trevelyan, Sir George. *A Vision of the Aquarian Age.* Walpole, NH: Stillpoint Publishing, 1984. An inspired guide amid troubled times.

Vaughan, Francis and Roger Walsh, editors. *A Gift of Peace.* Los Angeles: J.P. Tarcher, Inc., CA, 1986. Selections from A Course In Miracles.

Synergy

> SYNERGY is the harmonious interaction of all parts with the whole. The word Synergy is derived from the Greek word syn-ergos, meaning simply "to work together."

Synergy is not a system of coercion or restraint, but one in which the elements spontaneously support each other and the system as a whole. Richer complexity, growth, and integration are the bonuses derived from Synergizing systems such as networking (see NETWORKING). High Synergy systems perform at peak levels, systems low in Synergy are chaotic and weak. Peter Russell, author of *The Global Brain*, describes one type of high Synergy system:

> An excellent example of a system with high synergy is your own body. You are an assortment of several trillion individual cells, each acting for its own interest, yet each simultaneously supporting the good of the whole.... If it were not for this high synergy, each of us would be just a mass of jelly, each cell acting only for itself and not contributing to the rest of the body.

> Synergy in an organism is the essence of life, and it is intimately related to health. When for some reason synergy drops....the organism becomes ill.

Human society today appears to be in a state of low Synergy and dis-ease. To correct this illness requires a "new thought" paradigm (see PARADIGM SHIFT) that encourages holistic, peaceful, humane, and non-exploitive approaches to living. A shift in awareness to a Synergistic world view would stimulate high levels of creativity, vision, and invention. This expansion of consciousness is fast becoming an evolutionary imperative.

Recommended Reading

Russell, Peter. *The Global Brain*. Los Angeles: J.P. Tarcher, 1983. A scientific and visionary statement of approaching world Synergy.

Transformation/Transcendence

> *TRANSFORMATION literally means to transform or restructure. It is a process of change in which higher levels of unity and unconditional love are integrated in one's personality and consciousness.*

> *TRANSCENDENCE is seeing beyond our "normal" unawakened state of awareness through the eye of enlightenment.*

From ancient times to present day, individuals have explored a variety of rhythmic exercises, oral repetitions, and spiritual practices to encourage the Transformative process in their lives. Personal Transformation systems abound, such as: yoga, alchemy, shamanism, meditation, relaxation through breath control, affirmations, dream analysis, modern psychotherapy, sensitivity groups, rolfing, running, chanting, isolation tanks, biofeedback, hypnosis, mystic teachings, karate and other body movement disciplines, mind altering drugs, and this list grows larger by the year. Human beings by their very nature are in a constant state of Transformation, although the degree and form with which this process occurs is as unique as the individual. No single discipline works for everyone.

True Transformation is not temporal but bestows long-lasting changes in personality and consciousness — *the butterfly cannot re-enter the cocoon.* The effects of Transformation have been described as "living fully," "whole-seeing," "joys of creative risk-taking," "freedom from childhood programming," "loving without expectation," "clear and sharp sensing," "feelings of kinship and unity," "conscious of one's consciousness," and "a sense of meaning."

These shifts in personal paradigm seek to integrate one's "many selves" and to transcend the "self-encapsulated ego." It is believed that through the process of Transformation divisions between mind and heart are healed and one's inner duality of masculine and feminine natures are reunited — in Buddhist literature this is called *sahaja*, "reborn together."

The catalyst for Transformation may be the painful experience of divorce, serious illness or accident, the death of a loved one, or job loss.

However, even the sudden success of promotion, marriage, or financial windfall can generate sufficient stress to demand new order. In *The Aquarian Conspiracy*, Marilyn Ferguson writes that we live in a state of hypnosis and build walls of avoidance and denial until we are shaken into wakefulness. She continues:

> *At the level of ordinary consciousness, we deny pain and paradox. We doctor them with Valium, dull them with alcohol, or distract them with television....*

Denial is the alternative to transformation. Ferguson outlines the four steps of transformation: (1) "Entry point" — a spontaneous trigger to question, to peek outside one's mind-box. (2) "Deliberate letting" — allowing new information, sensation and feelings to enter one's mind-box. (3) "Integration" — where search and exploration flower to form healthier, more holistic ways of being. (4) "Conspiracy" — the drive to communicate transformative experience with others, a uniting or synergy of self-lessness.

Transformative experience reflects light on the soul and guides one to a *new* knowing of the "center." This secret center, this "Mystery" is represented in mandalas, the alchemical marriage, sanctum sanctorum, the holy of holies, and the king's chamber in the pyramids. Transformation moves us closer to the Mystery, spiraling toward the center. "We sit around in a ring and suppose," wrote Robert Frost, "but the Secret sits in the middle and knows."

Recommended Reading

Anthony, Dick, Bruce Ecker, and Ken Wilber, editors. *Spiritual Choices: The Problem of Recognizing Authentic Paths to Inner Transformation.* Paragon House, 1987. Designed to help the reader recognize valid approaches to spiritual development.

Fields, Rick. *Chop Wood, Carry Water: A Guide to Finding Spiritual Fulfillment in Everyday Life.* Los Angeles: J.P. Tarcher, Inc., 1984.

Metzner, Ralph. *Opening to Inner Light: The Transformation of Human Nature & Consciousness.* Los Angeles: J.P. Tarcher, Inc., 1986. Required reading.

Sinetar, Marsha. *Ordinary People as Monks and Mystics: Lifestyles for Self-Discovery.* Mahwah, NJ: Paulist Press, 1986.

Smothermon, Ron M.D. *Transformation #1*. CA: Context Publications, 1982. Explores transformation of self, integrity states, the technology of creativity, transformation of relationships and business.

Tart, Charles T. *Waking Up*. Boston, MA: Shambhala Publishing, 1986. A transformative journey from "waking sleep" sto human potential.

Wilber, Ken, Jack Engler, and Daniel Brown. *Transformation of Consciousness* Boston, MA: Shambhala Publishing, 1986.

Unconditional Love

> *UNCONDITIONAL LOVE is born of the heart and not of the mind. In Dante's words, "it is the love that moves the sun and all the stars."*

Perhaps the clearest way to discern the meaning of Unconditional Love is to first state what it is not. It is not manipulation, domination, dependence, possessiveness, duty, pity, approval, cravings, lust, fear, jealousy, or judgment. Unconditional Love is not based on needs, desires, or personal tastes. It cannot be stolen or earned and it loves beyond that which offends one's individual biases. Unconditional Love is an open and vulnerable exchange. It calls for us to meet heart to heart, center to center, and not merely at our peripheries. This creative process lives in the present and lets things be. Unconditional Love simply *is*.

The channeled writings of Emmanuel state:

> *Love is all that exists*
> *All matter is formed by love.*
> *There is an organic love that*
> *speaks to everyone*
> *if they could but hear.*
> *A leaf holds together for love.*

Unconditional Love does not require us to say yes when we need to say no. Unconditional love does not require the condition of liking something we dislike, or meeting someone's expectations. It extends beyond these boundaries in the limitless world of the heart. The heart can love another's struggle and humanness regardless of that person's actions or beliefs. The alchemy of genuine love blesses all who are touched by its transformative power. Avatar Meher Baba believed that to have loved one soul is like adding its life to your own.

Recommended Reading

Buscaglia, Leo. *Love.* New York: Fawcett Crest, 1972. Endearing and enduring.

Hendricks, Gaylord. *Learning to Love Yourself.* New York: Prentice-Hall, Inc., 1982. Creative approaches to increasing your willingness to love yourself.

Keyes, Ken Jr. *A Conscious Person's Guide to Relationships.* Coos Bay, OR: Love Line Books, 1979.

Moss, Richard M.D. *The I that is We: Awakening to Higher Energies Through Unconditional Love.* Berkeley: Celestial Arts, 1981.

Welwood, John, editor. *Challenge of the Heart.* Boston, MA: Shambhala Publishing, 1985. An inspiration.

Unity/Oneness

> *UNITY and ONENESS are terms used to capture the universal truth of wholeness.*

There are seemingly many dualities (see DUALITY THEORY) in our world — look closer however and you will find they are but parts of the greater whole. Emmanuel says it this way:

> *Around the distortion and the duality of your earth is the Oneness of God's Love. There is an undivided world that is truly governed by Love and Light and Truth.*

If you want to find duality in your world, humankind has made it easy; the body and mind, spirit and matter, good and evil. However, these are not dualities — only aspects of the Love force in constant creation.

"I and the Father are One" it was written long ago. If we believe in the seeming duality of good verses evil, we bring the word *enemy* to our reality, creating opposing forces. The enlightened (in-Light) consciousness of Unity and Oneness enables us to free ourselves from the misleading concept of good and evil and brings Light (see LIGHT) to our reality.

"I in you and you in me" was also written. The consciousness of Oneness is the basis of love. We are one. Bringing this consciousness to our reality will shift our attitudes toward other nations, races, religions, earth's ecology (see ECOLOGY/STEWARDSHIP), and even the universe itself to that of Unity. This concept of Oneness can become a working principle for our world. Emmanuel tells us, "The universe was not made for anything other than to unite...the two extremes of consciousness. And when we unite them, we find that the two extremes are exactly the same thing: one whole, unique and innumerable at the same time."

Recommended Reading

Bach, Richard. *One*. New York: Silver Arrow Books, 1988. A novel surrounding the Oneness of all lives.

Rodegast, Pat, and Judith Stanton. *Emmanuel's Book: A Manual for Living Comfortably in the Cosmos.* New York: Some Friends of Emmanuel and Bantam Books, 1985.

Rodegast, Pat, and Judith Stanton. *Emmanuel's Book II.* New York: Some Friends of Emmanuel and Bantam Books, 1989.

Satprem. *Mother or the Divine Materialism.* New York: Institute of Evolutionary Research, 1979.

Watson, Lyall. *Lifetide.* London: Hodder and Stoughton, 1979. Examines the concept that "we are all One."

White, John W. *The Christmas Mice.* Walpole, NH: Stillpoint Publishing, 1984. A powerful message of peace and Oneness written for children.

Unity —A Way of Life, Unity Village, MO. Monthly magazine.

Vision/Visionary

> *A VISION is an image which originates outside ego consciousness. One experiencing a Vision believes it is occurring in the outer world, when in actuality, it springs from one's unconscious mind.*

> *A VISIONARY is a person who senses the future as universal and timeless. A Vision is a spontaneous psychic experience, therefore, many sensitives also find they are Visionaries.*

People who have experienced a Vision are often profoundly affected by their experience. Visions, like dreams and hallucinations, are extremely vivid images which may seem convincingly real. They usually appear in symbolic form in an attempt to integrate the inner and outer worlds, spiritual and material, microcosm and macrocosm (see MICROCOSM/MACROCOSM). A Vision may be induced by meditation or prayer, certain mind altering drugs, high fever, flashing lights, or deprivation of sleep, food, or sensation.

Mystics teach that thought forms are captured in time but that visions transcend time. Lama Anagarika Govinda, an American born Lama of the Tibetan Buddhist tradition and mystic, denoted that visions are timeless because they originate from a higher dimension.

The history of humanity is rich with reports of Visions and Visionaries. Talented men and woman, such as Kennedy, King, Emerson, Elliot, Dickenson, DaVinci, Madame Curie, Schweitzer, Einstein, Gandhi, Gorbachev and Sadat have inspired and ushered our evolution with dreams and Visions of the future. Western transcendentalist, William Blake, was a Visionary in the truest sense, seeing beyond the assumptions and accepted limits of society, religion, and the illusion of time. He expressed his experience of an all-inclusive mystical Vision in these famous lines:

> *To see a World in a Grain of Sand*
> *And a Heaven in a Wild Flower*
> *Hold Infinity in the palm of your hand*
> *And Eternity in an hour.*

Recommended Reading

Bryant, Dorothy. *The Kin of Ata are Waiting for You.* Canada: Moon Books/Random House, Inc., 1971. An enthralling Visionary novel.

Cayce, Edgar, et al. *Visions and Prophecies for a New Age.* Virginia Beach, VA: A.R.E. Press, 1981.

Jung, C.G. *Memories, Dreams, Reflections.* New York: Random House, 1963. Fascinating autobiography from a fascinating Visionary.

Keen, Sam. *Voice and Visions.* New York: Harper & Row, 1970. Discussions with Joseph Campbell, Carlos Castaneda, Roberto Assagioli, and other present day Visionaries.

Lutyens, Mary. *Krishnamurti: The Years of Fulfillment.* New York: Avon Books, 1984. An illuminating biography of an enigmatic Visionary.

Weber, Renee. *Dialogues with Scientists and Sages: The Search for Unity.* New York: Routledge and Kegan Paul, Chapman and Hall, 1986. David Bohm, Krishnamurti, the Dalai Lama, Rupert Sheldrake and other Visionaries share their views on consciousness, creation, space, time, energy, and our place in the universe.

Visualization

Visualization

VISUALIZATION is just like seeing except it is done with the mind's eye or imagination, using that part of the brain which registers thought, memory, ideas, and the subjective rather than the physical eye. Visualization is used for the purpose of influencing both external and internal conditions.

Gerald Jampolsky, founder of the "Center for Attitudinal Healing" maintains that what we see *without* is a reflection of what we have already seen within our mind. Dr. Jampolsky instructs his patients with catastrophic illnesses to visualize themselves in the most positive and healthy form they can, a process by which conscious energy is spread to every cell. This particular energy produced during Visualization is thought to have a mending or healing quality.

Creative Visualization is applied in many areas of medicine, science, and research. This technique is also regularly employed in competitive sports and in training for the Olympic Games to encourage an athlete's optimum performance. Visualization can be used for achieving personal success in any area of one's life:

1. Establish a goal or desire based upon what you want in life: a new home, an automobile, a raise in salary, a more successful relationship or perhaps a new one. Write your goal down, speak it aloud to establish it consciously as well as in the subconscious. Use exact language to assure total meaning. You might use a picture, an ad, or article to help pin-point the details.

2. Daily reference is important. To cement the goal in your subconscious, take a few minutes every day to imagine or Visualize the desire fulfilled. In the case of a new car, picture yourself buying and driving this prize. Visualize the color, the style, and the feeling you'll have owning a brand new automobile — Visualize it as real.

3. Act as if your goal has already been met. This is not as difficult as it sounds. The act of Visualizing creates a certain state of mind which directs you toward appropriate behavior and response. Visualize yourself having, being, or doing exactly what you desire. Imagine taking your friends for a ride in your new car; imagine driving down the freeway or a country road on a rainy day or a starry night.

4. Feel yourself unseparated from your desire. Draw your completed goal to you by visualizing its progression from idea to image to physical reality, and then accept its manifestation (see MANIFESTATION).

Another form of Visualization is known as Guided Visualization, a technique used for relaxation or to relieve stress. It works by providing the imagination with a peaceful place for retreat — it is quite like meditation (see MEDITATION) in that it renews or revitalizes energy flow.

The peaceful place can be one you have invented for yourself, one you actually remember, or one which another leads you through in your imagination. You can even record a favorite Visualization on cassette tape and listen to it regularly. The following Guided Visualization is an example. Read it over, then sit or lie back, close your eyes and picture yourself there. Release the day's tension and relax to the sights and sounds of your inner mind:

It is night. Waves of emerald sea break on a shoreline in a distant land and rhythmically splash the rocks below you. The soft sound of a tide-pool clearing its shelves of sand rushes in your ears. You feel a warm breeze around your shoulders as you breathe in the sea-fresh air. You walk along the mirrored shore and bend to pick up a pink scalloped shell. Your fingers trace the scalloped edges to feel its texture. Above, a shooting star slices across a crescent moon and you stop to dream a wish. Peace-filled and content, you walk, knowing you can return here at any time.

Recommended Readings

Achterberg, Jeanne. *Imagery in Healing: Shamanism & Modern Medicine.* Boston, MA: Shambhala Publishing, 1985. Healing through Visualization.

de Jim, Strange. *Visioning.* San Francisco: Ash-Kar Press, 1979. Inspiring guided Visualizations.

Fezler, William. *Creative Imagery.* New York: Simon & Schuster, Inc., 1989. Creative imagery using all five senses for ". . . a blue-print to your spiritual growth."

Gawain, Shakti. *Creative Visualization.* New York: Bantam Books, 1978. Instructive guide for Visualizing a new future.

Gawain, Shakti. *Living in the Light.* San Rafael, CA: Whatever Publishing, 1986. More guidance.

King, Serge. *Imagining for Health.* Wheaton, IL: The Theosophical Publishing House, 1981.

Samuels, Mike, M.D., and Nancy Samuels. *Seeing With the Mind's Eye.* New York: Random House, Inc., 1975. An in-depth study with techniques for practical use.

Index

A

B

C

The Authors

Paula Slater and Barbara Sinor are sisters whose interest in the field of consciousness studies began early in life. As children, encouraged by their mother to share metaphysical insights, they learned to look within for truth and guidance. Paula and Barbara together completed their graduate studies at John F. Kennedy University in the Graduate School for the Study of Human Consciousness, each focusing on specific areas of study.

PAULA SLATER is an accomplished freelance writer and artist. Her interviews with leading-edge thinkers and personalities of the New Age and her expansive articles on metaphysics, creativity, and parapsychology have appeared in numerous national magazines. Her present writing endeavors include a multi-dimensional novel entitled, *Star Peace.* Paula is widely known for her work as a fine artist and professional illustrator. The painting found on the cover of *Beyond Words* is just one glimpse of her unique artistic, visionary talents.

BARBARA SINOR is a transpersonal therapist in private practice in Northern California. She continues to challenge and stretch the minds of those who seek her counsel. An accomplished writer and published poet, Barbara is busy completing *Gifts from the Child Within,* which introduces Re-Creation,© a transpersonal counseling technique focusing on the inner child and the recovery process for those who grew up in a dysfunctional family. Ms. Sinor plans to continue her writing, teaching and counseling while exploring the magic found *beyond words.*

Grateful acknowledgement is made for permission to reprint from the following:

Abbott, Edwin A. *Flatland.* New York: Penguin Publishing, 1987.

Allen, James. *As a Man Thinketh.* New York: Grosset and Dunlap/Putnam Group, 1984.

Avery, Jeanne. *The Rising Sign.* New York: Doubleday & Company, Inc., 1982

Bach, Richard and Leslie. *Illusions: The Adventures of a Reluctant Messiah.* New York: Dell Publishing Company, Inc., 1981.

Berkeley Holistic Health Center. *The New Holistic Health Handbook.* Lexington, MA: The Stephen Greene Press, 1985.

Bolen, Jean, M.D. *The Tao Of Psychology: Synchronicity And The Self.* New York: Harper & Row Publishing, Inc., 1979.

Boyne, Gil. *Transforming Therapy.* Westwood Publishing Company, 1989.

Capra, Fritjof. *The Tao Of Physics.* New York: Bantam Books, Inc., 1984.

Cayce, Edgar. *Auras: An Essay On The Meaning Of Colors.* Virginia Beach, VA: Association for Research & Enlightenment, 1973.

Childress, David Hatcher. *Lost Cities Of Ancient Lemuria And The Pacific.* Stello, IL: Adventures Unlimited Press, 1987.

Cole-Whittaker, Terry. *What You Think Of Me Is None Of My Business.* San Diego, CA: Oak Tree Publications, Inc., 1979.

Coxhead, David. *Visions of the Night: Dreams.* New York: Crossroad Publishing, 1982.

Dante. *Dante's Divine Comedy.* Yorktown Heights, NY: Belser, Inc., Publishers, 1987.

Eddington, Sir Arthur. *Science And The Unseen World.* London: Macmillan Publishing Company, 1979.

Fawcett, Lawrence and Barry Greenwood. *Clear Intent.* New York: Prentice-Hall, 1984.

Ferguson, Marilyn. *The Aquarian Conspiracy: Personal And Social Transforma-tion In 1980's.* Los Angeles: J.P. Tarcher, 1987.

Ferrucci, Piero. *What We May Be: Techniques For Psychological And Spiritual Growth.* Los Angeles: J.P. Tarcher, Inc., 1982.

Foundation for Inner Peace. *A Course In Miracles.* Tiburon, CA: Foundation for Inner Peace, 1975.

Gibran, Kahlil. *The Prophet.* New York: Alfred A. Knopf, Inc., 1923 and renewed 1951.

Harman, Willis, and Howard Rheingold. *Higher Creativity.* Los Angeles, CA: J.P. Tarcher, Inc., 1984.

Heisenberg, Werner. *Physics and Beyond.* New York: Harper & Row Publishing, Inc., 1971.

Hitchcock, Helyn. *Helping Yourself With Numerology.* New York: Parker Publishing Company, Inc., 1972.

Jeans, Sir James. *The Mysterious Universe.* New York: Cambridge University Press, 1933.

Kusher, Lawerence. *Honey From The Rock.* New York: Harper & RowPublishing, Inc., 1977.

Laubach, Frank. *Prayer: The Mightiest Force.* Christian Books Publishing House.

Lazaris. *The Sacred Journey: You And Your Higher Self.* Palm Springs, FL: NPN Publishing, Inc., 1987.

MacLaine, Shirley. *Out On A Limb.* New York: Bantam Books, Inc., 1983.

Meeker, Joseph. *Minding The Earth; Thinly Disquised Essays On Human Ecology.* Joseph W. Meeker, 1988.

Meher Baba. *Discourses.* North Myrtle, NC: Sheriar Press, 1987.

Meher Baba. *The Everything And The Nothing.* North Myrtle, NC: Sheiar Press 1976.

Metzner, Ralph. *The Laughing Man.* A magazine. Lower Lake, CA: Dawn Horse Press.

Metzner, Ralph. *Opening To Inner Light: The Transformation Of Human Nature and Conciousness.* Los Angeles: J.P. Tarcher, Inc., 1986.

Mitchell, Edgar D. *Psychic Exploration.* New York: The Putnam Berkley Group, Inc., 1974.

Morris, Richard. *The Nature Of Reality.* New York: McGraw-Hill Book Company, 1987.

Moss, Thelma. *The Probability Of The Impossible.* Los Angeles: J.P. Tarcher, Inc., 1974.

Murphy, Joseph. *The Power Of Your Subconscious Mind.* NJ: Prentice-Hall, 1963.

Rengel, Peter. *Seeds Of Light.* Tiburon, CA: H.J. Kramer, Inc., 1989.

Ring, Kenneth. *Heading Toward Omega: In Search Of The Meaning Of The NDE.* New York: William Morrow & Company, 1985.

Roberts, Jane. *The God of Jane: A Physic Manifesto.* Englewood, NJ: Prentice-Hall, 1981.

Roberts, Jane. *The Nature of Personal Reality.* Englewood, NJ: Prentice-Hall, 1974.

Roberts, Jane. *The Seth Material.* Englewood, NJ: Prentice-Hall, 1970..

Rodegast, Pat and Judith Stanton. *Emmanuel's Book.* New York: Bantam Books, 1985.

Russell, Peter. *The Global Brain: Speculation On The Evolutionary Leap To Planetary Consiousness.* Los Angeles: J.P. Tarcher, Inc., 1983.

Sayers, Dorothy, translator. *The Divine Comedy.* New York: Watkin Loomis Agency, 1950.

Strieber, Whitley. *Communion: A True Story.* New York: William Morrow & Co., 1987.

Singer, Peter. *Animal Liberation.* New York: New York Review, Inc., 1977.

Taylor, Richard. *Metaphysics.* New York: Prentice-Hall, Inc., 1983.

Toben, Robert, and Fred Wolf. *Space, Time And Beyond.* New York: Bantam Books, Inc., 1975.

Vaughan, Francis. *Awakening Intuition.* New York: Anchor Press/Doubleday, 1979.

Vernon, P.E. *Creativity: Selected Readings.* New York: Penguin Publishing, 1970.

Watson, Lyall. *Supernatural.* Great Britain: Hodder & Stoughton, 1973.

Watson, Lyall. *Lifetide.* Great Britain: Hodder & Stoughton, 1979.

Watts, Alan. *The Book.* New York: Pantheon Books, 1966.

Wilber, Ken. *Quantum Questions: Mystical Writings Of The Great Physicists.* Boston, MA: New Science Library, 1984